Book of Tea

Annie Perrier-Robert is vice-president of the *Association Française de la Presse Gastronomique et Touristique* and a member of the *Académie Française du Chocolat et de la Confiserie*. A specialist in the history of gastronomy, she has written over twenty books, including *Le Chocolat* ("Chocolate") and *Les Biscuits"* ("Biscuits").

All Christine Fleurent's photographs are taken from *Plaisirs de thé* ("The delights of tea") by Michèle Carles and Gilles Brochard.

Annie Perrier-Robert

Book of Tea

HACHETTE
Illustrated

Contents

Introduction

As soon as it reached the West, this delicate beverage from Asia, where it was used as a better quality alternative to plain water, aroused the boundless enthusiasm of lovers of the exotic, as well as the fierce hatred of puritanical minds, who considered it a substance likely to alter the activity of the brain and detrimental to physical health. The French writer Honoré de Balzac (1799–1850) was among those who condemned tea as being a "modern stimulant", in the same way as coffee and chocolate. Today, such debates have been consigned to history, together with the elitist image that was long associated with drinking tea. "By means of tea, the Orient penetrates middle-class drawing rooms; by means of coffee, it enters the brains" said Paul Morand. As a result of its expansion, the mysterious infusion became a part of social interaction, a pretext for pleasant get-togethers with friends, family or intimates, as in the famous "Tea for Two". Today, tea can claim to be universal. Depending on the traditions regarding its preparation, it takes on unusual, surprising, but always sophisticated flavours.

The three cups of tea

Marked with poetry in its very essence, both in its distant origins and in its ritual, tea has been a source of inspiration to poets the world over. Like many others, the writer Jules Barbey d'Aurevilly (1808–1889) was sensitive to this beverage and to its symbolism. He dedicated a poem to tea, published in the posthumous collection of his works entitled Poussières (1897). This hymn to tea is an appropriate opening for this book

"I was alone. She was at the dance last night, wearing a gown the colour of the moon. A faithful heart captured in a changing petticoat! For I was thinking of an opalescent petticoat while watching the pale gold of the tea as, light and burning hot, it flowed into my cup – burning hot and light, like one's first love!"

"And it was amber and not gold, this liquid gold was so pale, and that is why, being such a romantic soul, I saw floating in it a reflection of the skirt of indeterminate hues, when it suddenly darkened, this clear beverage, and, no longer burning hot, turned from pure gold to bright red in the diaphanous Sèvres porcelain – red like the blood of a man who is no longer shedding his first drops of blood in love, but who is emptying his whole vein into the wound of a second love!"

"But it was at the third time of looking that it darkened with even greater foreboding, streaming more slowly into the porcelain chalice – thick, black and steaming like the mortal blood of this bull, whose blood is given, so it is said, to King Cambyses to drink, in order to kill him. No longer gold! No longer light! No longer scarlet! But the dark, deep and bitter purple – the vein emptied of the very last drop of his life! His soul! The whole heart burnt in its most intense flame – in the inextinguishable fire of a final love!"

"And will you believe it? Yes, you will believe it. This dark colour – so far removed from the pale hues of the shimmering, clinging satin of the opal skirt – was the one that reminded me most of the chaste gown of the angel clad in rays of light, who bore my life on his wings and carried it to heaven!"

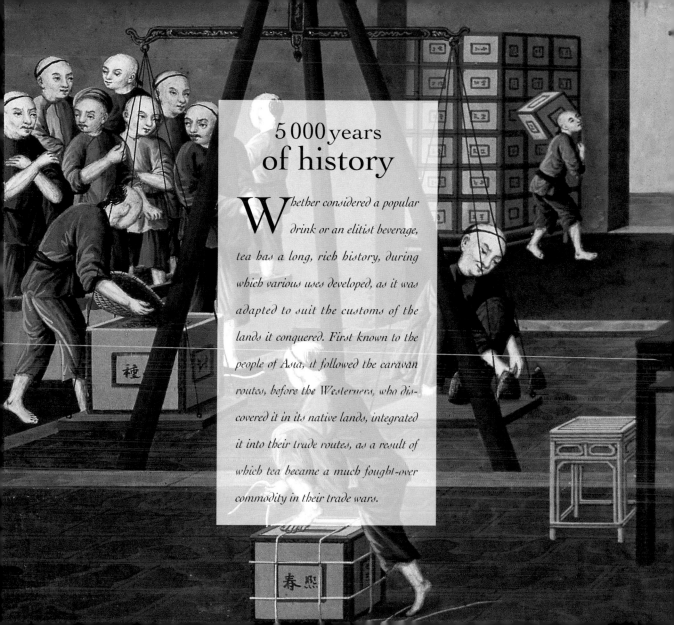

5 000 years
of history

Whether considered a popular drink or an elitist beverage, tea has a long, rich history, during which various uses developed, as it was adapted to suit the customs of the lands it conquered. First known to the people of Asia, it followed the caravan routes, before the Westerners, who discovered it in its native lands, integrated it into their trade routes, as a result of which tea became a much fought-over commodity in their trade wars.

The poetry of origins

The beginnings of tea as a drink in China remain shrouded in mystery. Some sources say they lie in the 6th century BC, while others put it considerably earlier. Be that as it may, it did not acquire its name of ch'a *until the early Han Dynasty (206 BC – 8 AD).*

THE "DIVINE HARVESTER"

The discovery of tea is said to go back to Shen Nung, the deity with a bull's head and the father of agriculture, who ruled in China in about 2737 BC. Resting at the foot of a bush and being thirsty, he is said to have asked a servant to boil him some water. A few leaves fell from the bush into his cup. Seduced by the sweet and restorative beverage thus produced, he is said to have ordered this plant to be cultivated throughout the land.

Above
The legend is shown in the decoration of another legend, the lidded cup (*chung*). The lid served to retain the flavour of the tea and, when barely raised, to prevent the leaves from leaving the cup and entering the mouth when drinking the tea.

Previous page
Inside a Hanist shop.

THE BUDDHIST MYTHS

Another legend concerning the origins of tea told by the Indians and the Japanes presents Bodhi Dharma, son of an Indian king, who went to preach Buddhism in China. To carry out his mission successfully, he is said to have taken an oath not to sleep for seven years. One day, however, he felt himself being overwhelmed by

AUX INDES

Tea may have been known in India before China.

sleep and was only kept awake by the leaves of the tea bush that he chewed. Filled with wonder at the restorative properties of the plant, his disciples are said to have then cultivated it and spread the word about it throughout the Middle Empire.
A second version claims that, ashamed at having succumbed to sleep despite himself, Bodhi Dharma then cut off his eyelids, tea bushes taking root where they fell.

THE THREE EPOCHS OF TEA

In the 8th century, under the Tang Dynasty, tea was already a popular drink in China. It came in blocks, the leaves being crushed, then pressed into moulds and dried by the heat from a fuel fire. It was at this time that Lu

The art of tea

"After exchanging formalities, the grandmother princess lost no time in asking for a cup of her famous tea. The young nun served her some herself, bearing an exquisite KangXi polychrome porcelain of the very best period, made of fine, translucent clay and with sumptuous, clear colours, on a lacquer tray decorated with begonias, dragons, clouds and engraved *zusong* characters. The tea that the porcelain pot contained was of one of the most precious varieties known as the "eyebrows of Laozi".
"What water did you use to make the tea?" asked the grandmother.
"Rain water collected last year," replied the nun [...]."
Coa *Xueqin, Dream of the Red Chamber*, 18th century

Yu wrote his work, *Ch'a Ching* ("The Tea Classic"). The "master of tea" associated the drink with the celebration of life, inherent to Chinese thought, and surrounded it with a specific ritual, a reflection of an inner ethos extolled by the followers of Confucius and which generated harmony. Under the Song Dynasty, at the instigation of Emperor Hui Tsung (1101–1124), tea in block form gave way to tea in powder form, which led to a new method of preparation, the tea being whipped into "froth of jade". This custom is still retained in the Japanese tea ceremony.

Advertising tells the story, with a little imagination…

During the Mongol occupation (1279–1368), the air of culture
that had surrounded tea was forgotten, only to resurface with the
Ming Dynasty (1368–1644). Since that period, tea has been
prepared as an infusion. The Chinese were at that time already
familiar with black tea, green tea and *Oolong*.

THE SPREAD OF TEA

Although tea (*ocha*) had reached Japan during the first centuries
AD, it was only in the 8th century that the Japanese experimented
with growing tea – it must have become widespread during the reign
of Emperor Saga (786–842). Initially, the Japanese used tea in block
form, then, towards the end of the 12th century, at the instigation of
a Zen monk called Elisai, they switched to powdered tea (*matcha*),
thus laying the foundations for a custom that the monk, Sen no
Rkyû, would go on to raise to the status of a philosophy.

The conquest of Europe

Although, in the 16th century, many western travellers mentioned the favourite drink of the Chinese and the health-giving properties of the infused "herb", it was not until the 17th century that the first tea leaves were introduced in Europe, probably by Jesuit missionaries.

Top right
Three wives of wealthy Dutch merchants taking tea, 17th-century engraving.

COMPANY MONOPOLY
The Dutch were the first to import tea to the West. During the first decade of the 17th century, in order to obtain tea at a low price, the Dutch East India Company claimed in China and Japan that the Europeans had plants, namely sage and borage, that were broadly on a par with tea as far as therapeutic properties were concerned. That way, it was able to exchange sage for tea, at the rate of one pound of sage for three pounds of tea. It retained the tea monopoly until the end of the 1660s, when England, which had banned products coming from Holland from entering its territory, gave the East India Company the monopoly for the Chinese tea trade.

A DELICIOUS DRINK
France discovered tea at the same time as England, but did not greet it so enthusiastically. In fact, although in France it became a rare and expensive commodity – the French government applied heavy taxes to tea, which were not lowered until 1784 – the English rapidly began to consume tea in great quantities,

which carried on rising: over 2 million kg in 1769, compared with only 65 kg in 1699! The Dutch and the Danish turned out to be equally heavy consumers. The most common quality of tea at that time was *bohe* tea.

AN UNCHANGED METHOD OF PREPARATION

Tea was already being prepared using the "recipe" that we know today. As François Massialot explained in *Nouvelle instruction pour les confitures*, 1692, "The usual way of preparing Tea is to boil in a vessel for that purpose sufficient water for the desired number of doses, & when it boils, you remove it from the heat to add the Tea leaves, in

Above
Full Moon Teapot, by Mariage Frères. In Europe, tea was slower to appeal than coffee.

The unforgettable Boston Tea Party

Was tea the origin of the process that would culminate in the proclamation of the United States of America? In 1773, the East India Company acquired the monopoly to sell tea in America and the smuggler traders from New England rose up against this privilege awarded by London, all the more so because it was accompanied by high customs duties. Thus, in the same year in Boston where the protest movement against the English "tyranny" was virulent, they threw into the sea the cargo of three ships that had just come into port – 342 chests of tea in all! The Crown responded with repressive laws. The American War of Independence soon erupted.

Clippers contributed to the spread of tea in Europe in the 19th century.

TRAITÉS NOVVEAVX & CVRIEVX DV
CAFÉ DV THÉ ET DV CHOCOLATE
Composéz
Par Philippe Sylvestre Dufour

Above
Engraved
frontispiece
to Philippe
Sylvestre
Dufour's
famous *Traitez
nouveau et
curieux…*
(Lyon, 1865)

Opposite
Tea being
delivered to a
merchant, 18th-
century Chinese
print.

proportion, that is to say, one dram, then cover the
vessel and leave your Tea to infuse for the third part of a
quarter of an hour. During this time the leaves will sink
to the bottom of your Tea pot or cafetière, & the water
will take on its colour; pour into your cups, put half a
teaspoon of Sugar in each, then drink as for Coffee."

A TRICKY EXPEDITION

Initially, the only Chinese port open to foreigners was
Canton. The black tea route was extremely long. From the
province of origin, it took several weeks for the chests to
reach Canton, on board "tea boats" for most of the journey,
but also carried on men's backs across the mountains.
Once at the port, they were loaded onto western boats.
The journey to the West provoked real competition
between the countries. In the 19th century, the clippers,
large sailing ships chartered for the opium trade, were used
to transport tea, a delicate commodity that did not travel
well. Hence the need for rapid transit…
Each year, the "tea
race" earned the
winner a prize
awarded by the
London merchants.

Tea as a vegetable

Scotland acquired a taste for tea
much later than England. This
explains the misunderstanding
that occurred in 1785, when the
Duchess of Monmouth sent a
pound of tea leaves to one of her
relatives, who, not knowing how
to use them, chopped them up,
boiled them and served them as
for spinach.

Right
From Tomsk to Irkutsk, a tea caravan in winter.

Opposite
In Peking at the foot of the old city walls.

The tea caravans

*T*he caravans have long criss-crossed the planet. Tea was one of the major trading commodities of these mobile companies, on which big business depended.

A guarantee of quality

In the 19th century, tea transported by caravan was considered to be better than tea that travelled by sea in view of the harmful effects of the water and the humidity on this delicate commodity. Rolled less tightly and often broken, it had a distinctive aroma. So it is not in the least surprising that Alexandre Dumas affirmed that "the best tea is to be found in Petersburg and throughout Russia in general". The caravans transported Chinese tea, particularly *peko* tea from northern China, to Russia, where considerable quantities of it were sold each year at the Nizhni Novgorod fair.

The "ship of the desert"

This is the nickname given by the Arabs to the camel, the merits of which the French naturalist Buffon (1707–1788) acknowledged when he wrote: "Gold and silk are not the real riches of Asia. It is the camel that is the real treasure of the East". Powerful, docile and quick, this valuable animal can carry extremely heavy loads, far greater than can be borne by even the strongest horse.

Special packaging

Chinese tea was exchanged for cotton and woollen fabrics. The tea chests carried by the caravans, known as *tsibiki* in Russia, were generally made of wood, covered in cane or bamboo, and, once they arrived at the Chinese-Russian border, were then tightly wrapped in cowhide, bare side facing outwards. This protection meant the tea arrived in good condition and undamaged, for, even in Russian territory, the chests were transported by camel as far as Orenburg and in carts as far as the Volga.

On the way out...

Even the word "caravan", which comes from the Persian *karwân* ("business insurance"), is a good indication of the nature of the association that was thus created. Moving as a group was intended to protect against all the various dangers that were often faced, such as bad weather, poor roads and bandit attacks. The merchant exporters had to band together to run their commercial business successfully. Men and beasts of burden followed each other in never-ending lines. The creation of roads, the appearance of the railway, the rapid expansion of inland canal systems and of other means of transport hit the caravans hard, even in the most desert-like regions. The tradition has managed to continue only in a few regions where nomadic ways of life persist, such as with the Bedouin of Arabia and the Tuaregs of the Sahara.

Below
Long lines of camels used to cross the steppes of eastern Europe and central Asia, working for the tea trade.

The democratisation of tea

In the 19th century, the "modern" tea trade gradually began to establish itself. Tea was widely consumed in northern Europe. Across the Atlantic, New York was the most important market and the second largest in the world after London.

Together with Le Havre, the port of Marseille has long ensured imports of tea to France.

A DOUBLE IMAGE

"The vast room is cold. The colonel's wife pokes the fire in the hearth and comes to the tea table.

'I clearly do not expect you two gentlemen', she says, 'who, with truly chivalrous heroism have braved the storm to visit us, to content yourselves with our humble ladies' tea. Miss Margaret will prepare you the good drink of the north, which stands up to the most terrible weather…'" This extract from a tale by E.T.A. Hoffmann (*A mysterious visitor*) illustrates the image many people in Europe often had of tea: a delicate infusion, which only women could enjoy. For the men, punch was *de rigueur*.

The same author chose to set another tale (*The sequence of things*) in the "aesthetic tea of madam consistorial president Veehs", during the course of which "a dozen ladies, all grandly dressed, are seated in a semi-circle in the centre of the salon", listening, either inattentively or attentively, to a young tragic poet running through his works. This was the other dimension of tea, the drink of witty conversation and elegant meetings, of this world of "literary salons" that Balzac described as the "golden cycle where the Muses steal away the Hours".

CAFÉ DES GOURMETS TRÉBUCIEN

LE THÉ

A tea soirée

"Mme de Bargeton was generally praised for the care she
lavished on this young genius
[*Lucien*]. Once her conduct
had been approved, she want-
ed to obtain general sanction.
She publicised throughout
the *Département* a soirée
with ice-cream, gateaux
and tea, a great innovation
in a town [*Angoulême*]
where tea was still sold by
chemists as a drug to help
with indigestion. The crème
de la crème of the aristocracy were invited to hear
a major work to be read
out by Lucien."

Honoré de Balzac,
Illusions perdues, I, 1821

POPULAR IN ENGLAND

Meanwhile, the English, of all
social classes, had taken up tea
unreservedly, consuming some
3 million kg of it. This was the
same quantity as in the previous
century, but for a much greater
population, and hence an indication
of a growing fraud, which
involved the addition to the tea of
ash and blackthorn leaves and used
and re-dried tea. As a result, in
London in 1818 more than 20
grocers were convicted of selling
adulterated tea. Until 1834, trade
with China was ensured by the East
India Company under the

A mysterious alchemy

"That evening, like most evenings when he found himself in Valognes and when his wandering fish did not drag him away, he was going to spend the evening with the de Touffedelys girls. He took his tea caddy and his teapot, and there he made his tea in front of them, those poor primitives, to whom emigration had not given those astonishing tastes such as 'the love of these small leaves rolled in hot water', which was not a patch, they said, mouths full of wisdom, 'on *the green liqueur* of Chartreuse as a remedy for indigestion'. Tireless in their astonishment, they recalled at a given point the animal attention of beings that cannot be educated, watching each evening with their two glazed clay eyes, wide open like bull's eyes, this *original* de Fierdrap proceeding to make his accustomed infusion, as though he were engaged in some terrible alchemy!"

Jules Barbey d'Aurevilly,
Le Chevalier Des Touches, 1864

provisions of the monopoly. "Tea has become a commodity of absolute necessity, and our government gives generously to an association of private individuals the right to a monopoly over it, and to sell it at more than 200% of its true price!", as you could read in the *Edinburgh Review* at the time.

CONTROVERSY IN FRANCE

Apart from a few towns such as Bordeaux, which were open to customs from elsewhere, primarily England, tea continued to be a beverage for those "with good taste" until 1814, when it gradually overcame the objections of middle-class morals. It still had many detractors. But it was the taste for coffee, extremely widespread in France, which single-handedly did for tea. As a result, France consumed a hundred times less tea than England.

Below
Tea is the traditional drink of Siam (Thailand) – here in the 19th century.

THE RAPID EXPANSION OF PLANTATIONS

Until the 19th century, the tea consumed in Europe came exclusively from China. This supremacy would gradually decline, as tea growing became more widespread. Tea was first grown in India in 1834, Java in 1838, Formosa around 1870, Malaysia from 1874, and Ceylon (Sri Lanka) in 1876, the island's coffee bushes having been ravaged by disease. Attempts were made to acclimatise the tea bush in various places, including Guyana, Martinique, Sicily and Egypt, but they were in vain. The tea bush cannot be removed from the heavens that saw its birth…

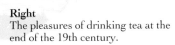

Right
The pleasures of drinking tea at the end of the 19th century.

The global nature of tea

From the many "gardens" of Darjeeling, producers of the "champagne of teas", to the vast tea estates of Sri Lanka, whose reputation is firmly established, tea growing has continued to spread across the world. There have been plantations in Africa, the South Sea Islands (such as Australia and Papua-New Guinea) and even in South America, namely Argentina and Brazil, since the middle of the 20th century.

AN ASIAN TRADITION

Four countries – China, India, the island of Sri Lanka and Kenya – account for some two thirds of global tea production. Although China had long been the largest tea producer and Europe's preferred supplier, it saw the gradual emergence of formidable competition. It remains a top tea producer but is now second in the world for, despite coming late to tea growing, India is currently the number one producer. The plantations are concentrated in the north east, in the Assam plain, on the banks of the Brahmaputra and in the Darjeeling region, on the southern slopes of the Himalaya, as well as in the south-west, on the plateaux of the Nilgiri Hills. Sri Lanka is the third largest producer. Its plantations are grouped together in the centre of the island, in the mountainous regions of Nuwara Eliya and Kandy, as well as in the Uva and Dimbula districts.

1900, Paris Universal Exhibition. *Un thé sur la Seine.* Watercolour by Maurice de Thoren.

AFRICAN TEA

Although first introduced to Africa at the end of the 19th century, tea was not actually grown there until the 1920s, and then mainly in Mozambique and Southern Rhodesia, before spreading to other countries, such as Cameroon and Burundi. The development of tea growing in Kenya, where it was first cultivated in 1925, was as extensive as the British influence there was strong. The fourth largest producer in the world, Kenya became the largest exporter in 1996.

TEA DRINKERS

The number one customer for these tea producing countries is western Europe, followed by North America and Africa. Consumption is clearly very high in the Anglo-Saxon and Muslim countries, whereas tea consumption in France continues to be modest.

The tea experts

Tea brokers act for buyers and sellers, sometimes for both at once. They test and value teas for the tea auctions that are held in some producer countries, including India, Sri Lanka, Kenya and Bangladesh, as well as in London, and which deal with three-quarters of the global tea trade. The rest is sold through direct dealings between the importers and planters or tea brokers.

The other tea experts, tea tasters, are to tea as oenologists are to wine. They can recognise, appreciate and analyse teas. What is more, they often have the talent to develop new blends: these blenders are real creators

First planted in 1860 on the flanks of the Himalaya, at between 1,000 and 2,100 metres above sea level, the tea gardens of Darjeeling produce the "king of black teas".

The beneficial properties of tea

"Dressed in a fur-lined gown, seated on a long Chinese couch covered with carpet, he insistently offered us scented green tea, excellent, he asserted, for dissolving fatty foods [...]."

Han Suyin,
The Mountain is Young

Semi-fermented tea (*Oolong*) is considered to be good for the digestion. Even today, chemist shops still sell a pressed Chinese tea (*Tuocha*).

A PERFECT REMEDY

Attributing beneficial properties to tea is in no way recent. In times gone by, in China and Japan, monks viewed tea both as a stimulant conducive to meditation and a sort of elixir of life. To drink tea is to extend your life expectancy…

What is more, this idea underlies the centuries'-old use of the beverage in Japan. It is true that it helped combat sleep, the first quality attributed to it according to legend. It also had other uses, however, including combating the humours and abscesses, quenching thirst and toning up the heart.

CONTROVERSIAL SUBJECT

Throughout the 17th and 18th centuries, tea was at the centre of the "health talks" given by learned scholars, and even in the 19th century it retained an image that was debatable to say the least. Did not a certain Zimmermann describe it as "dirty Chinese washing powder"? Fortunately, this condemnation, which went so far as to assert that tea was a factor in the "degeneration of the species", was not generally felt. Most agreed that, provided it was consumed in moderation, this "pleasant" beverage presented no danger – provided, that is, you preferred black tea to green tea and flower-bud

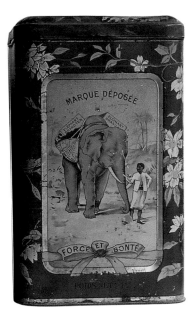

It was in 1827 that Oudry isolated an alkaloid, theine, which has analgesic, tonic and diuretic properties.

pregnant women; as a result of its fluorine content, it helps prevent dental caries; and it contains an enzyme that has a positive effect in cases of arterial hypertension.

rather than leaf tea. The controversy continued to be hotly debated until late in the 20th century.

A USEFUL PLANT

Closer to home, analyses and research carried out by eminent pharmacists and doctors have surfaced the actual qualities of tea and its dietary role. Green tea contains three times as many minerals as *Oolong* Chinese tea, even though it too is rich in these elements. It has also been shown that the tannins in tea are far more active than Vitamin E in slowing down the degeneration of the cells; its zinc content is good for

Does tea prolong life?

In the 19th century, there were a few people who believed this to be the case. Take, for example, the following report in the *Revue britannique* in 1826:
"In Penrith, in Cumberland, a woman, called Mary Noble, has lived primarily on tea for sixty-five years, and she is now one hundred and seven years old. [...] Her health and energy have been preserved to the extent that she still walks without the aid of a stick."
Elsewhere, in a study published in London in 1827, *The Sure Method to Improve Health and Prolong Life*, an English scientist mentioned tea and cited a certain Jean Hussey, of Sydenham, who lived to be one hundred and nineteen years of age and who, for fifty years, contented herself with dining on "mint tea sweetened with a little honey."

Of teas and
tea bushes

Full of subtlety, the world of tea is similar in some respects to that of wine. Different estates produce specific 'vintages' and the quality of the leaves and the special treatments that are applied create particular varieties of tea. There is thus a multitude of factors relating to the categories and grades used to determine how tea is classified, depending on its origin, time of picking and leaf size.

A precious bush

The tea bush grows naturally in the mountainous regions of southern Yunnan (China), northern Burma, Assam and also in northern Thailand and Laos. But almost all of the varieties grown (jat) have originated from the first plants native to China or Assam.

7,000 shoots produce one pound of saleable tea.

A MISTAKEN IDEA

Long ago, following the example of Linnaeus, it was believed that there were two species of tea bush, one green *(Thea viridis)* and the other black *(Thea bohea)*. In the 19th century, this assertion was proved to be mistaken. In the 1840s, the East India Company entrusted the English botanist, Robert Fortune, to discover the secret of Chinese tea and, while travelling through China, he was able to prove that: "Black teas and green tea, which are generally forwarded to England from the northern provinces of China, come from a single, unique species, and their differences in colour and flavour, amongst other things, are solely the result of their different methods of preparation."

REQUIREMENTS

The tea bush *(Camellia sinensis* or *Thea sinensis)* belongs to the Theaceae family. If left to its own devices it could grow up to 15 metres high but, when cultivated, it is shaped into a shrub with its top flattened to form a 'picking table'. Undaunted by such treatment, its leaves, dentate and lance-shaped, resemble feathery down, before turning smooth and glossy. Tea needs heat and humidity. Moreover, it is happy only on the hillsides in light, rich and well-drained soil. Tea is therefore found growing in the zones situated between 43° North and 27° South. It is grown at altitudes of up to 2,500 metres and its productive life spreads over 50 years or even longer.

THE QUALITY OF THE PICKING

As its name suggests, the 'imperial' picking was reserved for the emperor of China and involved the removal of only the terminal bud.
It was carried out on one single

Left
A close relation, the camellia belongs to the same genus as tea.

day each year, at sunrise, between the end of the February moon and the beginning of the March moon. The pickers – young virgins – had to wash their hands seven times before slipping on silk gloves and cutting using golden scissors. This ritual has long since disappeared.

Now, the terminal bud is harvested together with its nearest leaf ('imperial' picking), or the terminal bud together with its two closest leaves ('fine' picking), or alternatively, for tea of inferior quality, the terminal bud plus the next three or more leaves ('classic' or 'coarse' picking).

TEA SEASONS

The flush (or picking) begins when the plant is between three and five years old. The tea is picked by hand by women,

Opposite page
Plantation in Malaysia

Right
A branch of a tea bush with its fruit capsule containing seeds.

The flower resembles the wild rose, while its scent is reminiscent of jasmine.

On the Darjeeling road

"Kursiong is in the middle of tea country. As far as the eye can see, all the mountain slopes are covered by plantations that would call to mind the hillsides of the Rhine and Moselle if the miserable tea bush, pruned right back by industrial processes, could rival the broad branches seen in vineyards in terms of elegance. Tea, which is found growing wild in the neighbouring province of Assam, prospers here just as well as it does in China. It flourishes even at altitudes of 1,800 metres, but it is the plantations situated below 1,000 metres that produce the highest yield. Moreover, the abundant rain on the southern flanks of the Himalayas renders irrigation totally unnecessary, even when the ground slopes to such an extent as to prevent water from accumulating."

Count Goblet d'Alviella,
Inde et Himalaya,
Souvenirs de voyage, 1880

usually three times a year. The 'spring' flush (in April and May) produces the most sought-after teas. The second, 'summer' flush (from June to August), provides coarser and more aromatic teas. Finally, the third, 'autumn' flush produces inferior teas with a more marked aroma. As the sap is concentrated mainly at the outer edges of the tea bush, the nearer the leaves are to the terminal bud of each branch, called *pekoe* (from the Chinese word *pak-ho*, meaning "feathery down"), the better the quality of the tea. Also, the younger the leaves, the finer the tea.

TRADITIONAL METHOD OF PREPARING BLACK TEA
Once picked, the leaves are quickly processed. They are first *withered* in a well ventilated place for between 16 and 24 hours to dehydrate and soften them and reduce their tannin content. They can then be *rolled* (this is done lengthways) to rupture the cells, thereby allowing the various constituents to mix.

The strength of the tea depends on how tightly it is rolled. The leaves are then *fermented* in a hot (25° to 27° C) and very humid atmosphere for two or three hours. This gives them their brown colour and further reduces their tannin content. The leaves are then *desiccated* (or *roasted*) at 90° C for about 20 minutes. When it has turned black, the tea contains less than 5% water. Finally, the *grading* process separates the leaves by quality, and the tea is packed in aluminium-lined plywood chests.

Fine black teas

"Barely had the steaming urn been placed at the centre of the table than you could see all the faces light up; the nervous system seems to be soothed by the mere anticipation of the pleasures that this sweet beverage will bring to each of those present. Conversation becomes more piquant and rapid. People discuss, but without disputing."

Revue britannique,
September 1828.

IN THE NAME OF THE WORLD

The Chinese call it 'red tea' because of the colour of the infusion. It is the Europeans that call it 'black tea', because of the dark colour produced by the fermentation process. These teas, which come in various qualities and strengths of aroma, are the ones Westerners consume in greatest quantity. They are the principal tea grown outside China and Japan. The black teas of Sri Lanka enjoy a good reputation, as do those of India, especially Assam and Darjeeling.

FROM A CHINESE VIEWPOINT

The main Chinese teas are *Yunnan* ("south of the clouds"), which originates from the region of the same name, and *Keemun*, from Anhui province, the subtle and light altitude tea. *Pur Erh*, produced in Yunnan, is an extremely old tea, as was used in making tea blocks. Although fermented for a shorter period than a traditional black tea, it is not considered to be an *Oolong* tea. Black teas can be smoked. With their rich, complex character, smoked teas, which Fujian province has made into a speciality, date back to the 17th century. Legend has it that, after soldiers from the imperial army had occupied the tea factory, the freshly picked leaves had to wait to be processed and, wishing to meet their delivery commitments, the workers thought it a good idea to speed up the drying process by burning pine wood. Today, although spruce is used instead of pine, the artisan tradition continues.

In Montpellier

"I learned the name of the fashionable café as a result of a maid's indiscretion. Off I ran hither, but alas! My wishes knowing no bounds, I asked for some hot water. I had in my pocket a supply of excellent tea from Kiancha, which had never seen the sea, a present from the amiable Mme de Boil…"

Stendhal,
*Mémoires
d'un touriste*

Thé noir CEYLAN — Galaboda, OP1

Thé noir, ASSAM first flush — Bamonpookri, TGFOP

Thé noir. CHINE — Yunnan d'Or

Thé noir fumé CHINE — Lapsang souchong

Thé noir CEYLAN — Somerset Pekoe

DARJEELING Thé noir - first flush — Castleton, SFTGFOP1

DARJEELING Thé noir - second flush — Jungpana, SFTGFOP1

DARJEELING Thé noir - Autumnal — Arya SFTGFOP 1 «Rose d'Himalaya»

Opposite page
Tea picking in India

Left
A selection of the most famous black teas

Page 41
Women picking tea in Sri Lanka

Pondicherry in the 18th century

"Breakfast is served at nine or ten o'clock; then the Mistress of the house, with a table laid with cups before her, presides until one o'clock over the ever-changing circle of Visitants, and has nothing to do but pour the tea. Lunch is followed by the Siesta, a sort of second night that lasts until four o'clock; you get undressed and go to bed. From five o'clock to eight o'clock, tea starts up again, and often provides the sole source of conversation; because once the Vessels of Europe have left, people no longer have anything to say, unless love has provided some adventure, about which the victims of this God will be the first to make a joke."

Abraham-Hyacinthe Anquetil-Duperron, *Zend-Avesta*, vol. 1

A MATTER OF PRESENTATION

The leaves can be whole, broken or even powdered (known as *fannings* or *dust*), the latter being used for tea bags. The

Le Thé — *Torréfaction, le Five o'clock.*

difference in presentation has absolutely no effect on the quality of the tea. Broken tea simply has a greater yield than whole-leaf tea, so infuses more quickly and is generally coarser.

A STRICT HIERARCHY

There are different qualities of whole-leaf tea. When only the terminal bud *(pekoe)* and the first two leaves are picked, the tea is called *Orange Pekoe (O.P.)*. This tea with its well rolled leaves has a mellow fragrance and delicate flavour. In China, it is sometimes called *Congou. Flowery Orange Pekoe (F.O.P.)* comes from exactly the same picking, but from younger shoots, and has more *tips* (the delicate tips of the buds) than *Orange Pekoe. Pekoe*, on the other hand, which is similar to the previous teas but is not so fine, has fewer or sometimes even no tips. *Souchong* uses the third or fourth leaves. Its large leaves, rolled up lengthways, are used for smoked Chinese teas, such as the famous *Lapsang Souchong*.

A similar hierarchy applies to broken teas: *Broken Orange Pekoe (B.O.P.)* contains no tips, while *Broken Tea (B.T.)* is made from pieces of flat (non-rolled) leaves.

A Chinese tea capital

"I found myself at present in the environs of Fokien, that vast black tea region. I noted a great number of tea plantations, generally in the foothills and also in the villagers' gardens. At around ten o'clock in the morning, we came to Tsong-gan-hien, a large town situated at the heart of the same region that produces the black tea [...]. The town is full of large *tea-hongs*, where the black teas are sorted and packaged for foreign markets. All the coolies that I came across during the course of my travels in the mountains came to get work here. Tea merchants from all the regions of China where this product is consumed or exported come here to buy their tea and arrange for it to be transported."

Robert Fortune,
A Journey to the Tea Countries of China, 1852

THE BLENDER'S ART

The range of teas has, over time, been further enhanced by blends created by experts. In this way, the harvests from various estates or the produce from various gardens, or even various pickings, are combined. Even black and green teas are often combined, the aim always being to obtain a specific tea, the flavour of which must then be made to last. One of the most common such teas is *English Breakfast*, a blend of black teas from India and Sri Lanka. And last, but by no means least, in the blends category come the flavoured teas.

Right
Darjeeling selimbong with its silver tips

THE AGE OF TRICKERY

Sensitive to light and humidity, tea quickly loses its flavour. In the 19th century, teas spoiled in transit were not, however, always thrown out. Although it was impossible to regain their flavour and aroma, some less scrupulous people worked to reinstate their normal appearance. The first such conjurors worked in England to metamorphose black tea into green tea using clever compounds, such as the lead chromate associated with Prussian blue, indigo, turmeric or copper salts. Some tricks were easy to detect: a bluish black tea infusion betrayed the presence of campeachy wood, for example. To see through some other tricks required quasi-scientific investigation, however, thus allowing the fraudsters to act with impunity.

Special teas

Coming half way between black tea and green tea, semi-fermented tea originated in China – in the provinces of Guangdong and Fujian, to be precise – and in Formosa (Taiwan). As for the white tea passed down from Imperial China at the beginning of the Song Dynasty, it has become extremely rare.

LEGENDARY ORIGINS

Although better known by the name of *Oolong* (or *Wulong*), semi-fermented teas have also been called *bohea*, *bohe* or even *bou*. The word *Oolong* ("black dragon") actually comes from a lovely Chinese legend. Having noticed a mellow scent, a picker went up to the tea bush from which it came. A black serpent was coiled in the bush. The man felt no fear of it, however, and picked a few leaves, as a result of which he made an exquisite drink.

INCOMPLETE FERMENTATION

Oolong teas, which the Chinese consider to be the best teas in the world, undergo only a brief fermentation period. In China, *Oolong* tea accounts for only 12% to 15% of production, whereas in Formosa it reaches 60% to 70%. The long leaves are kept whole and then rolled. These teas have a distinctive, fruity flavour, rich in nuances, together with an extremely delicate aroma. The most famous *Oolong* teas come from Formosa, where the plantations are concentrated in the north and north-west of the island. Although they have long been greatly appreciated in the United States and are increasingly gaining in popularity with the French, they are not well known in the West.

Below
Little known in the West, white tea is a 'rare' drink.

Above
Darjeeling, in India, also produces semi-fermented teas.

FAMOUS WHITE TEAS

The province of Fujian in the south-east of China, where, in the 19th century, tea made the ports of Fuzhou and Amoy (Xiamen) rich, has the almost exclusive rights to white teas.

Bearing the seal of special quality, these teas, with their silvery white leaves coated with white down, owe their special character to the fact that they are only withered after picking, before being dried in another process. With their fresh taste and delicate aroma, they outrival all other teas.

Opposite page
Oolong tea (above) is infused in a very small tea pot and served in small cups (below). The leaves are used three or four times in succession.

Imperial green teas

Unlike black tea, green tea does not go through a fermentation process. China and Japan are the major producers and consumers. Although less frequently exported, green tea is also found in Formosa (Taiwan) and in northern India.

Opposite page The Japanese green tea ritual.

An elitist tea

"Green tea (young-leafed) is the Chinese Château Lafite. It is drunk only in the homes of the aristocracy, having been picked specifically for them by young children or virgins with gloved hands. The lower classes have to make do with black tea, of which there is no shortage and which is quite readily available on the streets."

Baronne Staffe, end of the 19th century

PRECIOUS TEAS IN CHINA

Green tea is a real tradition in China. The provinces of Anhui, Jiangsu, Zhejiang and Jiangxi are the main suppliers, while the province of Hunan with its rare teas should also be mentioned. The freshly picked leaves are placed in heated iron bowls to roast. They are then rolled by hand and dried in hot air, these rolling and desiccating operations being repeated until the optimal degree of dryness has been attained. Chinese green tea has a delicate flavour, subtle aroma and a

A Chinese speciality, manufactured green teas are 'worked' by hand to form shapes such as bouquets, stars, buds and pearls. The poetry of the shapes is associated with the pleasures of the palate.

more or less marked bitterness. The best-known varieties include: *Gunpowder*, with its rich fragrance, the extremely young leaves of which are rolled into tight balls or 'pearls'; *Chun Mee* ("Precious Eyebrow"), the leaves of which are rolled up lengthways; and *Lung Ching* ("Dragon's Well"), with its flat, non-rolled leaves.

JAPAN, THE KINGDOM OF GREEN TEA

Wherever tea consumption enhances the art of living, there you will find green tea. The plantations are mainly on the southern island of Honshu and on the islands of Kyushu and Shikoku. The manufacturing process follows the same principles as in China, except that it is steam-heated and often machine-rolled.

Leaf tea *(Ryokucha)* tends to be used to make an infusion and comes in a wide range. *Sencha* is without doubt the most popular tea. Made of leaves picked in the first (spring) or second (summer) harvest, it can be either a superior or extra fine quality tea for special occasions, or an ordinary grade tea for everyday consumption. It is at one and the same time both sweet and slightly bitter in flavour, with a very subtle aroma. *Gyokuro* ("jewel dew", known in English as "jade dew") is considered to be the best green tea in the world. Produced from the first young leaves picked from best bushes during the first (spring) harvest, its leaves are larger than those of *Sencha* tea, and it is reserved for distinguished guests. It has a fuller, richer and less bitter flavour than that of *Sencha* tea and is usually served with a small, sweet cake.

Above
An everyday Japanese drink, *Sencha* tea is served from a one-handled teapot and poured into cups, filling them three-quarters full, until the pot is drained.

Below
Prepared green tea from the province of Anhui in eastern China.

Left
Powdered
Matcha tea,
ready for tasting

Below
Gyokuro tea set

The tea for the ritual

Central to the Japanese tea ceremony, *Matcha* is a powdered tea produced in the Uki and Shizuoka regions and demands the same degree of care as *Gyokuro* tea. Protected from the sun, the tender leaves are steamed and then dried, before being ground into a powder.

EVERYDAY JAPANESE TEAS

Bancha is a tea for everyday use. It is similar to an inferior grade *Sencha* tea. Its leaves, picked in the second half of the second harvest (at the end of the summer) or during the third harvest (autumn), are slightly larger, but produce tea of the same colour. It is served piping hot.

Hoji-cha is also an everyday tea. A brown-leafed roasted *Bancha* tea, it is therefore less rich in tannins and theine. With its distinctive flavour, it is *the* tea for the sick and for children. Like *Bancha*, it is drunk piping hot.

A favourite with the young, *Genmai-cha* ("rice tea") is drunk daily. It is a mixture of *Bancha* tea and grains of white rice prepared in much the same way as popcorn. Often enjoyed after a meal, it has a distinctive fragrance.

Other teas

Whether black, semi-fermented or green, teas are sometimes scented. The Chinese have long been masters of the art of blending aromas. People in the West are now taking over from them. Delicately scented with flowers or fruit, or providing the beneficial warmth of spices, these exotic flavours are an invitation to travel.

Known for centuries in Japan, instant tea first appeared in Europe towards the end of the 1950s.

Decaffeinated or detheinated tea containing less than 1 gram of theine per kilogram of tea is also available.

TEAS FOR THE TASTER

The tradition of flower teas goes back a very long way. In the past, men and women of fashion sometimes carried around with them boxes containing scented tea or a fine paste perfumed with tea. In the middle of the 19th century, Robert Fortune commented that some scented plants were cultivated for their flowers, which the Chinese blended with tea, particularly *Souchong* tea. This was particularly true of *Olea fragrans* ("sweet olive") and *Gardenia florida*. In China, you can find gardenia green tea, rose black tea and orchid tea, to mention but a few. The best-known scented tea in the West, however, is jasmine green tea, inseparable from Chinese cuisine. To make this, and other flower teas such as orange flower tea and camellia tea, the flowers are picked just before they open, then arranged in alternate layers with the tea leaves,

before being left in an enclosed place for several months. At the end of this period, the flowers are removed by hand, having sufficiently impregnated the tea with their fragrance.

DIFFERENT FLAVOURS

Clove, cinnamon, ginger, cardamom… teas flavoured with spices are much appreciated in India and have experienced increasing success in Europe since the 1970s. There are all sorts of fruit teas: red berry fruits, citrus fruit, exotic fruit, coconut… the list of flavours is endless. The best known of these teas is without a doubt *Earl Grey*, flavoured with bergamot. It is named after Earl Edward Grey, the British prime minister from 1830 to 1834, who made this ancient Chinese recipe so fashionable. It should be noted that, while bergamot is an essential ingredient of *Earl Grey* tea, the tea itself can be black, green or *Oolong*, and can come from China, Sri Lanka or elsewhere.

More recent innovations include honey, caramel and chocolate teas, sometimes spiced up with alcohol, such as rum, maraschino or whisky. And lastly, we come to 'health' teas, chosen for their low theine content and a response to the growing interest of the West in its physical health and vitality. This is true of some vitamin-rich fruit teas and of ginseng tea.

6ème Comte Grey

Opposite page
Jade Mountain blend, from Mariage Frères.

Tea in blocks

Block tea is traditional in China and is also used in Russia and Tibet. It is true that block tea is sometimes made from the leftovers produced from processing the leaves, which is then pressed into a compact whole, but compressed teas can also be made from whole leaves, pressed not only into simple blocks, but also into shapes such as pebbles, bars and even birds' nests. To use this type of tea, simply slice off the equivalent of 2 grams for each cup and boil in water for three minutes.

The legendary Japanese tea jars

In times gone by, superb translucent vases, white with a delicate green tint, were discovered on the seabed. These were priceless pieces, intended to hold tea…

An indefinable charm

Japanese tea enchanted the French novelist, Pierre Loti. In *Madame Chrysanthème*, he wrote: "I have a quite charming impression of Japan; I feel as though I have entered fully into this small, imagined, artificial world that I knew from lacquer and porcelain paintings. It is so good there! These three little women, seated, graceful, dainty, with their slanting eyes, their beautiful broad cockle shell buns, smooth and like varnish; and this landscape glimpsed from the veranda, this pagoda perched up in the clouds; and this precociousness that is everywhere, even in objects".

A much sought-after utensil

This sophistication is rooted in history. In the 18th century, the vases in which the Japanese would lock away their tea matched its quality both in terms of size and material, being large and made of ordinary clay for the ordinary variety of tea, and smaller and made of porcelain for the superior tea reserved for the emperor and his court. In the latter case, the ancient little

pots *(maats-uba)* were the height of sophistication. All these vases, with their short, straight necks, preserved the tea perfectly and even allowed its aroma to develop further over time. In his *Civic and Ecclesiastical Natural History of Japan* (Amsterdam, 1732), Kæmpfer reports an interesting legend regarding

Left
Lacquered wood tea-making kit (1826): three drawers, a container and a kettle

Opposite page
An attractively decorated tea jar from a 19th-century engraving

such vases, in particular the *maats-uba* made on the island of Mauri (Mauri-ga-sima), the most luxurious of all vases.

The wrath of the gods

The dissolute morals of the inhabitants of the island and their distrust of religion led the gods to wipe it off the map. The island chief, who actually led an exemplary life himself, was forewarned of this terrible punishment in a dream. "The gods told him to flee on the small boats as soon as he saw the face of two idols placed at the entrance of the temple blush. The king immediately told of the danger that threatened the island and the disaster that would of necessity strike it, but met with nothing but derision and distrust from his subjects for what they called his gullibility", explained Kæmpfer. In this context, some joker had the idea of painting the idols' faces red. The king immediately took this to be the warning he had been given and fled with his family by boat towards Foktsju, a province in southern China. It goes without saying that the population of the island was engulfed by the sea when the sentence of the gods was really carried out. That is how the famous Mauri potters and their tea jars, so famous throughout the country, came to disappear. From then on, a few rocks marked the site that, in mythological times, had been one of the centres of Japanese porcelain.

The tea
ceremony

Tea, although mocked by naturally boorish souls, will forever
be the preferred beverage of intelligent
people" affirmed the author, Thomas
de Quincey, at the beginning of the
19th century. That was probably true
in some western countries. Today,
however, tea is the most popular drink
in the world and its consumption is not
restricted to any one social group.

Photo F. Ozon., in L'Agenda du Thé, Le Chêne.

The right equipment

CHOOSING THE CONTAINER

The best teapots are the ones that retain heat well. For Chinese tea, it is advisable to use a glazed earthenware or porcelain teapot, whereas for Ceylon or Indian tea, which is coarser, it is better to use an earthenware, pewter or silver teapot, which is more in keeping with the period. The advantage of the pewter teapot is that it keeps the tea hot. Finally, it is advisable to reserve each teapot for its own particular tea, one pot for Chinese tea, another for Darjeeling, and so on. And most importantly of all, use these teapots only for making tea!

It is important to select tea with care, so it follows that the equipment used to prepare it cannot be chosen in haste. It is sometimes worth sacrificing elegance of form for lines which, although possibly less sophisticated, are better suited to the ritual that surrounds tea.

Top
The tea strainer remains true to its practical shape.

Right
The pure lines of traditional teapots.

TEA STRAINERS, SCOOPS AND BALLS

There is nothing more unpleasant when drinking tea than to feel bits of tea leaves on your palate, which is a very good reason to serve tea 'strained'. Some teapots have a filter to retain the tea leaves, which is removed when the infusion is ready. A common alternative is to use a suitable utensil in silver or stainless steel: either the common-or-garden tea-strainer that you place on top of the cup before pouring the tea or a small silver basket pierced with holes that is placed over the teapot spout and held in place by a sort of double-pointed pin. These accessories are based on the assumption that you put the tea straight into the teapot, which means that you cannot stop the tea infusing according to taste. As for the traditional tea ball that you put into the teapot, and which was invented by Westerners, it does not have much to recommend it, as the leaves are locked in and cannot release their full aroma. The same is true with regard to objects based on the same principle, such as the tea scoop. The best solution is in fact a sock-shaped fabric filter suitable for most teapots. The tea is totally unrestrained, and the pouch can be removed from the pot at will.

In the West, people often use tea bags to avoid the traditional strainer.

A few tips...

- If you are making just one cup of tea, use a tea scoop or a tea ball, placing it in the cup before adding boiling water.
- Put a sugar lump in the base of the teapot when it is not being used to prevent it from getting that unpleasant, stale taste.
- Do not wash your teapot with detergent – all it needs is a quick rinse. The tannin that is deposited on the insides of the pot should not actually be removed. If you really must get rid of it, use coarse salt instead.

Left
Only the 'tea pouch' allows the tea to release its full flavour.

A thousand and one teapots

"Speaking all the while, he served the tea with the self-conscious gestures of a strong man. And she was amused to see him handle the tiny porcelain teapot with its filter in the shape of a chalice with such unnecessary force."

Henri Troyat,
L'Araigne, *1938*

Below
This infusion vase from Ancient Greece resembles the teapots of today.

Centre
Sadler and Green invented printed decoration of glazed earthenware in England in 1750.

IMITATING CHINA

In the 17th century, with the first cargoes of tea, Europe discovered traditional Chinese stoneware teapots. Around 1670, Delft in Holland was probably the first place to make similar versions of them, in red ceramic stoneware. They sported reliefs of blossoming branches and dragons, with the decoration sometimes enhanced with coloured enamels. In the 18th century, these Delft teapots gained a following in England and in Meissen (Saxony) in Germany.

A very Chinese-looking enamel decoration.

THE PERFECTION OF THE CENTURY OF LIGHTS

As for the fine and translucent Chinese porcelain made of hard clay, it was impossible to imitate that in Europe until the process of manufacturing hard porcelain based on kaolin was perfected in Meissen in 1709. The first decades of the 18th century saw the golden age of chinoiserie for European manufacturers. The porcelain was adorned with superb, multi-coloured decorations

It's classicism and purity of line for these teapots, displaying English influences in soft-fired bisque, from Mariage Frères.

How to clean a pewter teapot

In her *Encyclopédie des Dames*, Mme Rouget de Lisle cites the following simple recipe: mix together the powdered 'weathered clay' or 'English red' with some oil. Place a small amount of this mixture on the teapot. Rub vigorously with a piece of flannel until the metal shines again. Then wash the pot in hot soapy water and dry. Finally, cover the pot with Spanish white, leave to dry and then buff up again using a chamois leather.

inspired by the Far East. In France, the 'rocaille' style, which broke right away from classicism, soon became popular with its floral motifs, scrolls and arabesques.

ENGLISH ELEGANCE

During the second half of the 18th century in Staffordshire, the ceramist Josiah Wedgwood patented his tea services, displaying his predilection for Antiquity and sophistication in his fine glazed earthenware with its creamy tones (known as *cream ware* or *queen's ware*) or colour (*cream-coloured ware*).
He also used red stoneware (*rosso antique*) to make tea sets for everyday use.

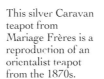

This silver Caravan teapot from Mariage Frères is a reproduction of an orientalist teapot from the 1870s.

The importance of colour

In his treatise on tea, Lu Yu was insistent on which bowls should be chosen in order to avoid changing the nature of the drink: the bowls should be quite shallow, straight, with a rounded base. A green-blue coloured glaze rein-forces the colour of the tea, while a yellow glaze makes a red tea turn rust-coloured, and a brown-coloured one black. He preferred ceramic bowls from Yueh Chou, "transparent like ice" and the colour of jade, claim-ing that this green alone could lift the colour of the tea. Probably an olive green glaze, some believe this may have been the first pale sea-green (celadon) porcelain. Produc-tion of this rare green-glazed ware, first appearing at the beginning of the Han dynasty, was particularly important during the Tang dynasty. The production site was revealed near Yu Yao in 1930.

— ✳ —

Left
Tall or short, round-bellied or slender, conical or geometric, richly decorated or plain, the teapot has evolved in line with fashion, with its spout and handle following this trend.

A HOMOGENOUS STYLE

It was not until the end of the 18th century, however, that the tea set first appeared, because, until then, cups and teapot did not match. From then on, a lidded sugar bowl and a milk jug completed the set. Moreover, the cup soon acquired a handle; the idea of adding this item goes back to the Chinese, who modified cups for export in this way. Before gaining its handle, the cup resembled a small, shallow bowl, and the plate on which it was placed could also be used to drink tea when cold.

ANOTHER FINE MATERIAL

From the 18th century, silverware began to appear alongside porcelain and stoneware teapots. That is when the VIPs became interested. Thus, in the 1770s, the

English architect and
ornamentalist, Robert Adam,
designed a range of silverware
teapots. In France, during the
Napoleonic era, Jean-Baptiste
Odiot and Henri-Auguste
Biennais made superb silver-
plate teapots.

**This page and
previous page**
Different
materials
(ceramic,
porcelain,
silverware)
for such
very different
tea sets!

A tradition and its rules

There are several rules that govern the preparation of tea, and which must be scrupulously observed if you want to obtain a top-quality infusion. It should be said that real tea lovers never neglect them.

Opposite page
At the turn of the 20th century,

'tea-time' was also a 'time for a chat'.

A few tips...

• If not serving the tea immediately, it is advisable to strain it to prevent it becoming bitter and stewed.
• If the tea is too strong, it is best to add hot water to the cup rather than to the teapot.

THE STARTING POINT
Carefully select the tea for the time of day when it is to be enjoyed. It is most important to use the correct amount. It cannot be left to chance: generally a rounded teaspoon per cup (2 to 2.5 grams) is the right amount. Adding 'one for the pot' will simply make the tea too strong.

GOOD QUALITY WATER
The type of water is essential. This observation is extremely old: Lu Yu devotes a long passage to it in his treatise. The tea master actually advocates using water from the mountains – from streams and lakes, but not from waterfalls or torrents; after that, water from rivers and then from wells is preferable. Modern living compels us to be more realistic. The water should be neither hard nor chlorinated. It is also preferable to use a neutral mineral water. Furthermore, the water that you put on to boil should be cold and, if using tap water, freshly drawn. Pour it over the tea as soon as it boils (95° C or more).

The etiquette of tea

"Tea is offered by the women of the house. One pours the tea into the cup, another will pass this cup on to the guest, holding the sugar bowl complete with sugar tongs in the other hand; while a third woman follows her with the milk jug and the plate of cakes. Brandy, rum or kirsch is brought for those who do not take milk.

The cakes eaten with the tea should not be dipped in the beverage; nor in any event should they be crumbled into the tea to produce a sort of soup. For tea as for coffee, the spoon should be placed on the saucer and not in the cup when you have finished drinking the infusion. This precaution successfully prevents accidents."

Baronne Staffe, 1894

Left
In days gone by, the kettle was used as illustrated in this engraving after a painting by Clémence Roth (1896).

A GOOD BREW

Beforehand, it is important to warm the teapot well by rinsing it out with boiling water. This should be done just before adding the tea leaves, so that they benefit from a gentle humid heat. Once the teapot lid has been replaced, it is important not to leave it to infuse for too long: the tea should be neither too light nor too dark, but an attractive amber colour. Generally, allow three to five minutes for Ceylon and Indian teas and five to eight minutes for Chinese tea. (The detailed infusion charts on page 126 help you time this more precisely.) At the end of this infusion time, stir the tea with a small spoon and then it is ready to serve. Tea is generally drunk hot, but some famous teas such as *Darjeeling* or the great Japanese green teas (*Gyokuro*) should be enjoyed warm, so that the heat of the water does not detract from their delicate flavour.

Left
Embroidered tablecloths and satin bows for this tea table, dressed in keeping with the fashion at the end of the 19th century.

Left
For tea lovers, each tea
should be served in its
appropriate container,
in this case Taiping
bowls (Mariage
Frères).

TO ENHANCE OR NOT TO ENHANCE

Although purists consider it sacrilegious to drink tea
any way except 'neat', some people prefer to enhance
it in a variety of ways. Depending on individual taste,
it may be with a slice of orange (never lemon, which is too
acid and 'kills' the flavour of the tea), a sugar lump
(always candy sugar as it does not impair the flavour
of the drink, and then only in some black teas, never
in the top-quality green or white teas), or perhaps a
drop of milk. Care should be taken, however, to ensure the
beverage is correctly mixed; the milk should be poured into the
cup before adding the tea. Milk should be served only with some
Ceylon or Indian black teas, such as Assam, which are the only
ones that can stand it.

The tea routine

Is tea the right drink for a particular time of the day? The English did not just invent afternoon tea. They were also responsible for the morning and evening cup of tea.

Above right
Old picture-postcard humour describing the pleasure of the morning cup of tea.

Below
Milk jug.

Opposite page
Small teapot.

'A NICE CUP OF TEA'

For the British, it starts as soon as they get out of bed, with the early morning cup of tea. The tea pot, which is usually topped with a tea-cosy, is accompanied by a small jug of milk and perhaps a couple of biscuits. The hot beverage ensures a refreshing start to the day. At breakfast, tea is traditionally served with toast, marmalade, cereals, orange juice and a hot dish with eggs.

THE 'CONTINENTAL' BREAKFAST

Tea is often used as a drink for when you are on the move. A breakfast tray must be laid out in a very precise way, if James de Coquet is to be believed: "The items must follow on from each other in a logical order. The cup must be in the front right corner. It is the advance guard, backed up by the teapot placed at its rear. To their left, the butter dish, the jam dish and everything that is butterable and jam-able. To the far left, the milk jug or lemon dish, the sugar bowl and the hot water jug. The latter is farthest away from the right hand since it is the last item to be used. Beneath the tea cup, I see a small plate, thanks to which it is possible to butter and spread your slices of toast."

Pretending to be dinner

"During this time, my lord busied himself preparing a pot of tea that would constitute his entire meal. To this end he devoted that meticulous attention, that grave importance that only an Englishman can; and, although the whole household was on their feet on this occasion, ready to do anything, ready to set themselves alight so that this tea would be perfect, my lord greeted the entire household with the stiffness which often characterises the Englishman of standing when travelling, at the inn and on the continent."

R. Töpffer,
Nouvelles genevoises

The English add a little cold milk to black tea, drinking it with or without sugar.

The Scots and the Irish add single cream.

As time went by

Since tea was first introduced to Europe, it has punctuated British daily life, whether at work or on holiday: a tea break in the morning; the traditional afternoon tea; and high tea, a meal in itself that can take the place of the evening meal. In the past, high tea was an opportunity to meet up with friends, chat or play games, such as whist. Today, it is a more intimate occasion that is usually restricted to family.

In the past, attractive silver spoons were used to serve tea from the caddy where the tea was kept.

Tea at breakfast in England, after a lithograph from 1840.

SERVING TEA IMPECCABLY

In France, afternoon tea, which was mainly taken by women and was often organised around a game, has quite a few devotees. Gisèle d'Assailly (*La Cuisine Considérée comme un des Beaux-Arts*, 1951) describes how tea should be served, no matter how unsophisticated it is. "We arrive at teatime: tea-and-a-chat, tea-and-bridge, tea-and-canasta… In private, the said tea makes its entrance on a trolley with its accompanying sandwiches and cakes. Sometimes it is laid out in the dining room and the teapot is the absolutely last thing to arrive, flanked by its jug of hot water. In any event, the silverware or pewter must be absolutely gleaming, while the serviettes or tablecloth must be embroidered or trimmed with lace.

Get-together over tea!

The tea smokers

"An English newspaper reports that the English are no longer content just to drink their afternoon tea – they *smoke* it!" It seems that it has become a fashionable craze to smoke green tea in the form of cigarettes. Many devotees of this extraordinary pastime are women of high standing and distinguished intellect. The blue smoke of the cigarette blends with the steam from the teapot, filling the drawing room with a scented mist. People chat more and take a particularly exquisite delight in speaking ill of their neighbour. And yet it was the English who reproached the French for their little Eastern tobacco cigarette and distanced themselves disdainfully from the cigar smoke. How absolutely shocking! *O tempora, o mores !* »
Henri de Parville,
Les Annales politiques et littéraires,
5th January 1896

Right
Menu for the *Au Louvre*. tea room.

Opposite page
Tea, engraving, 1829.

The signs of tea

"[…] on the small, low table, covered with a damask table-cloth […], there was a well-buffed teapot which you knew was half-full of cold tea, with the foreign glazed earthenware milk jug, the glass sugar bowl, the two fine large cups, the base of one of which was stained, with that little beige pool that remained there dotted with a dozen black spots, a flower plate on which were laid out four slices of toast, alongside that the nickel-plate device that had been used to serve them, the full butter dish, the jam dish and, on the metal of this teapot, an extremely bright ray of sunshine, gleaming like a star in the middle of all this darkness, because the blinds were just slightly apart, allowing a single ray to penetrate the room."

Michel Butor,
La Modification,
1957

Despite the passion of the slam and the American 'doubles', even the most enraged people will surely appreciate, during their passing 'demise', the appeal of these lowly pleasures of the palate… If there are a lot of people, the tea is placed on a tray at the edge of the table to make it easier to serve. The garnished tit-bits have pride of place: 'angry' prawns, rolled anchovies, slices of hard-boiled egg, the yolk of which is spread over a cornea of blushing tomato, little hands of asparagus with green fingers… there's plenty to bring a smile to your face! If you prefer sandwiches, decorate them with flag-shaped labels, erected as though on a newly conquered land, representing the sandwich filling: a goose for the pâté de foie gras, a pink pig for the ham, and so on."

Below
Chinese dinner service in Sèvres porcelain, from an engraving dating from the end of the 19th century.

The tea of hospitality

"The art of tea generally involves harmony between the Three Powers: the sky, the earth and man. The sky provides the sun's light, the mist and the rain that are necessary for growing tea; the earth provides the soil that nourishes the tea plants, the clay that is used to make all sorts of ceramics that are used for tea, the springs gushing from the rock that provide pure water for infusing the tea. To that, man adds the talent that links the tea leaves, water and the ceramics to produce an art full of appeal."
John Blofeld, Thé et Tao

A WELCOMING DRINK

Tea has always been offered in China as a sign of welcome. In 1864, A. Poussielgue confided in *Le Tour du Monde*:
"The custom of tea is no less widespread in the north than it is in the south. As soon as you enter a house, you are offered tea: it is the sign of hospitality. And you are served it in abundance; as soon as your cup is empty, a silent servant refills it, and it is only after you have drunk a certain quantity that your host will allow you to show the object you have brought." In the past, traders often used to offer their clients tea in their shop. Today, each meal starts with tea, whether at a restaurant or at someone's house. Tea is offered to guests at the end of a reception.

SERVED WITHOUT CEREMONY

The land of tea *par excellence*, modern-day China has remained faithful to the drink, but has somewhat sidelined the ceremony that used to surround the preparation and serving of powdered tea – a practice that was inherited by Japan, where it is still very much alive. In China, the customs may have gone, but tea is everywhere. Green and of varying degrees of sweetness, it is drunk piping hot, 'neat', without milk or sugar, mainly at the end of a meal and generally between meals.

In the ordinary run of things, it is not considered desirable to make a fresh pot using fresh tea leaves each time; the first infusion is given a new lease of life by adding boiling water. In the past, the used leaves were sometimes collected and sold on at a low price. And lastly, the tea can be flavoured in various ways, with jasmine, camellia or rose flowers, dried orange rind, nuts, pine kernels and apricot stones, for example.

Yunan-Fu shops

"They resembled theatres made of teak. Inside were lines of black boxes on which hand-painted golden dragons confronted each other. The merchant, an old mandarin whose chin sported a goatee beard, removed his hands from his sleeves only to weigh out the tea and calculate the price on his abacus. Buying tea was just as much pleasure as drinking it."

James de Coquet, *Lettre aux gourmets, aux gourmands, aux gastronomes et aux goinfres sur leur comportement à table et dans l'intimité*, 1977

Left
In China, it was customary to give this type of white metal teapot, with its symbolic silhouette, on the occasion of a happy event. This present was called *Jou-y* ("wish of good omen"). [19th-century engraving]

The green tea ritual

"This science or this art… of preparing a cup of tea in the most gracious of ways": that is how the American architect, Frank Lloyd Wright defined the Japanese ritual which had so fascinated him.

Below
Small cast-iron Japanese teapot.

Top right
Japanese nobleman.

Bottom right
Nothing is left to chance in the Japanese tea ceremony.

THE QUEST FOR PERFECTION

Long considered as a luxury product due to its rarity, and as a result the preserve of the elite, tea owes its unique role in Japanese culture to the Zen priests who, from the outset, were among its privileged consumers and made it into a vehicle for Buddhist philosophy. They did so by means of a ritual established in the 15th century by Shuko, who defined the rules of a tea ceremony *(cha-no-yu)* bearing the hallmark of Zen thinking. Following on from him in the 16th century, the priest Sen no Rikyu brought the 'Tea Ceremony' *(sado)* to the height of perfection, elevating this ritual of poetic entertainment to a true art, enabling the quest for serenity and self-realisation.

RESPECTING THE ETIQUETTE

The tea ceremony takes place within a structured environment, full of simplicity and harmony, grace and tranquillity: preferably in a pavilion reserved for this custom (see page 80), or, if that is not possible, in a special room (*tchashitsu*), the door (*nijiriguchi*) of which is so low that you have to duck to pass through it. Each element, each gesture, and the precise timing of them, has its own significance. The host uses a gong (*dora*) to indicate to his guests, assembled in a neighbouring room (*yoritsuki*), that they may enter the place for the ceremony. They then take their places and are served a light meal (*kaiseki*), carefully prepared for their benefit. About ten minutes go by, during which the guests leave the room and smoke or chat. The ceremony proper starts after this period of time (*nakadachi*) has elapsed.

Left
Even the packet of *Gyokuro*, the 'jewel' of green teas, looks exotic, sophisticated and enchanting.

Right
Bamboo whisk used to produce the 'froth of jade'.

The ceremony of old

The ceremony was even more rigorous than it is now: the water had to be boiled in an iron kettle over a little charcoal. Using a bamboo whisk, the tea was beaten in a bowl until the froth thus produced reached a specific level. The bowl was offered to the guest with prescribed gestures similar to the movements in a ballet. The guest drank his tea, performing a similar ritual as he did so.

MEDITATION AND SOLEMNITY

Ingredients: *Matcha*, the powdered tea made from the very best dried leaves. Equipment: one tea caddy *(tcha-ire)*, one small silk towel to wipe the equipment used to make the tea, a tea bowl *(chawan)*, a bamboo whisk *(chasen)* in the shape of a shaving brush and a bamboo or ivory tea scoop *(tchashaku)* used to transfer the powdered tea from the caddy to the bowl. The host prepares the tea with due solemnity: the powdered tea is combined with the hot water in the bowl, then the mixture is beaten with the whisk, producing a froth, which enhances the flavour of the tea. The bowl is given first to the guest of honour *(shokyaku)*, before being passed on to each guest, who takes a mouthful. The last guest *(tsume)* is responsible for wiping the bowl. It should be noted that the last guest is just as important as the first, because he has to help the host. Only an experienced person can fulfil this role.

EVERYDAY TEA

Today, green tea is such an essential part of Japanese daily life that, in addition to the

Previous page
In Japan, a tea ceremony conducted in the open air, but the rules still apply.

Left
Print by Shunman (1757–1820), Musée Guimet, Paris.

Below
This brazier is used to heat the water. In the foreground, the bamboo tea scoop.

'Tea cuisine'

The tradition of the tea ceremony led to 'tea cuisine', or *Kaiseki Ryori*. The word *kaiseki* is also used by some high-class restaurants to describe their cuisine. The dishes that they offer are similar to those that are served during a tea ceremony.

Better quality teas are served in light, white porcelain cups which show the beauty of the beverage to best effect.

Right
In a modern teahouse.

Opposite page
Tea plantations at the foot of Mount Fuji.

Matcha tea used for *cha-no-yu*, Japan produces a wide range of leaf green tea. Every traditional meal finishes with a cup of green tea, which is considered an aid to digestion. Any moment of relaxation involves a cup of green tea. Any welcome given with any degree of courtesy includes it. Whatever the circumstances, green tea is drunk neat (without sugar), to prevent it losing its bouquet.

A METICULOUS METHOD OF PREPARATION

To prepare green tea, the water has to be kept at boiling point for several moments, before allowing it to cool slightly in the case of the top qualities teas (*Sencha* and *Gyoruko*) so that it is at the correct temperature when it is slowly poured over the tea leaves: the better the quality of the tea, the lower the water temperature, the smaller the quantity of water and the shorter the infusion time.

It is best to warm the cups and teapot with hot water. When the infusion period is over, a small amount of tea is poured into each cup, from right to left, following the alignment of the cups. The operation is then repeated in reverse until the teapot is empty. This guarantees that the tea is shared out equally, both in terms of quantity and of quality. What's more, the tea leaves can be re-used two or three times.

Tea temples

There are places in Asia where the tea tradition is carried on. These are the 'teahouses', totally dedicated to the enjoyment of this precious liquid, which is both life-giving and popular, and which, in some countries, has acquired national drink status.

A real institution in China

In 1860, A. Poussielgue gave an interesting description of the Chinese teahouses in his work, *Le Tour du Monde*: "They are recognisable", he wrote, "from the workshop that takes up the back of the rooms and which is equipped with huge kettles, huge teapots, pipes and ovens that provide boiling water from the monstrous cauldrons that are as tall as a man. An unusual clock is placed over the workshop. It is made up of a thick stick of incense with equidistant markings, so that the wick indicates the passing of the hours as it burns."

The teahouse still plays an important role in the Heavenly Empire. Depending on the district and the clientele, it can be elegant, sophisticated, modest, suspect or even

Above
A teahouse on the banks of the Yang-Tse in China, at the very beginning of the 20th century.

sordid. In itself, it corresponds to the various types of drinks outlets that we know in Europe: somewhere to drink, somewhere to meet, somewhere to do business. Even today, though to a lesser extent, it continues to be a place of commerce where tea is omnipresent.

In Japan, deprivation and severity

The existence of teahouses also dates back a long way in Japan. In the past, it was possible to make out a whole hierarchy of such places, the differences being apparent in the interior layout and the garden, as well as the ceremonial nature of the service, rather than the exterior appearance. Thus the teahouses frequented by the aristocracy were more comfortable and elegant than those frequented by the middle classes. Furthermore, two types of aristocratic teahouse would exist side by side: on the one hand there were the teahouses reserved for the high nobility, while on the other there were those reserved for the *shoguns*, the military dictators that founded real dynasties in Japan from

Right
On returning from a boat ride, some

European travellers enter a teahouse.

LE VOLCAN FOUSI-YAMA

VISITE À UNE MAISON DE THÉ

the 12th to the 19th century. Nowadays, the tea ritual continues to take place, preferably in a pavilion dedicated to this purpose (*sukiya*). The place, often rustic, is simply decorated with a painted scroll and some flowers.

Left
Japanese teahouses seem unchanging,

both in terms of their décor and of the ritual that they adopt.

A global
drink

The Indians and the English take it with milk. The Orientals liven it up with mint. The Australians leave it to infuse for a long time, while the Irish enjoy it very strong. People in some countries add lemon, in others they season it with salt and butter or follow the Chinese custom and drink it 'neat'. It is drunk all over the world, made in a wide variety of ways using countless 'recipes'.

Around the samovar – Russian tea

Known in Russia since the 17th century thanks to the Mongols, tea was initially the privilege of Moscow and a few large towns. It was not until the 19th century that tea was widely consumed throughout the country.

Below
The rich vocabulary associated with the samovar in Russian is a clear indication of its importance.

Opposite page
Russian troops in a teahouse in Kishinev, from an engraving by G. Durand, 1877.

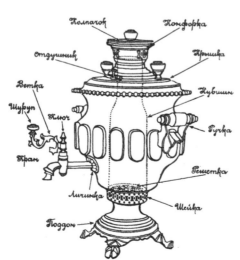

AN ESSENTIAL PART OF DAILY LIFE

"Evening tea was served to all the passengers, and the samovars, heated to excess, incessantly poured their boiling water over the concentrated infusion." This is one of the powerful images that the 19th-century French poet and author, Théophile Gautier, retained from his *Voyage en Russie*. The samovar and the tea caddy seem to be the key focus of Russian family life. There is not a novel or a play that does not make mention of tea being served. "She brought the samovar and, over a cup of tea, she was going to resume her interminable chatter about the court, when an armoured car stopped at the steps", as you can read in Pushkin's *The captain's daughter*.

A reviving drink

"Barely seated, the samovar appeared on the table accompanied by a tray bearing a Chinese teapot that would be the envy of any mandarin, with a skilfully measured portion of a tea that the head of the Heavenly Empire would certainly not have scorned, two large drinking glasses and a plate on which were arranged fine slices of lemon, as well as a small vase filled with cream. [...] This hot beverage, when one has just been exposed to great cold, is the most powerful tonic, the best one could possibly wish for."

M. Blanchard,
Un hiver à Saint-Pétersbourg,
1856-1857

For it is around this beverage that intimate scenes unfold, that business is transacted, that the difficulties of the soul are debated. In Imperial Russia, tea punctuates the day. The day starts with tea, served with bread, butter and sometimes cheese. It closes with tea too, two or three hours after dinner, with the last meal of the day, called 'evening tea' (*vietchernyï-tchaï*).

Whatever the time of day, the ritual is the same. Tea is traditionally served very strong in a porcelain teapot, and then diluted in the cup by adding boiling water from the samovar. The cup is reserved for the women, while the men are given a glass inserted into a handled holder made of more or

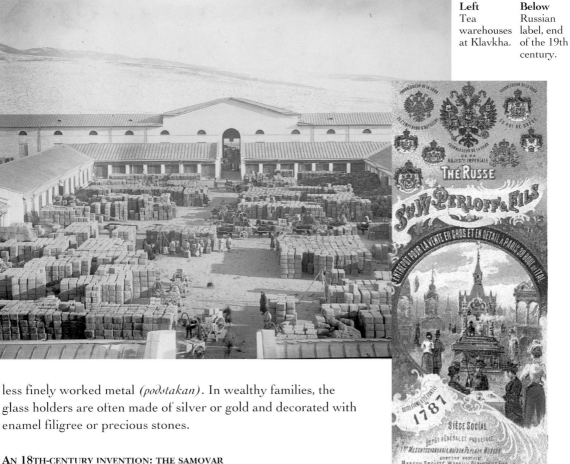

Left
Tea warehouses at Klavkha.

Below
Russian label, end of the 19th century.

less finely worked metal *(podstakan)*. In wealthy families, the glass holders are often made of silver or gold and decorated with enamel filigree or precious stones.

An 18th-century invention: the samovar

Today, the samovar is usually made of stainless steel or, better still, gleaming copper that is sometimes decorated. But in times gone by it could be made of silver or even gold. The most sought-after samovars were made in Tula, south of Moscow. Magnificent pieces of gold- and silverware were made for the

Previous page
The *traktir*, the traditional Russian tavern, was frequented by merchants, who discussed business there.

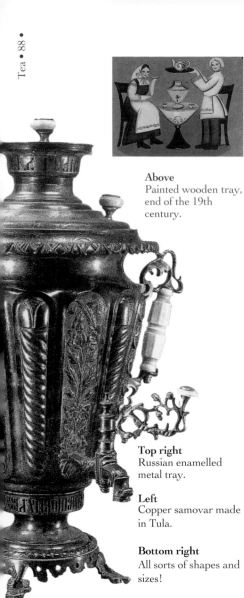

Above
Painted wooden tray, end of the 19th century.

tsars and for the court. A kettle in the shape of an urn, the appliance has a central chimney in which glowing charcoal embers are placed. These heat the water to boiling point, and is poured by means of a tap. During the ceremony, the teapot is placed to warm on the samovar. Unfortunately, while tea continues to be popular, the tradition of the samovar, which is nowadays always electric, is disappearing in favour of more modern appliances.

Top right
Russian enamelled metal tray.

Left
Copper samovar made in Tula.

Bottom right
All sorts of shapes and sizes!

SUGAR OR JAM?

Russian tea is made with black tea. In the 19th century, *Congo (Kong-fou)* was the most commonly used tea; *Pekoe (Pe-kao)* was also widely consumed. Some Russians preferred tea with a more subtle aroma, as indicated by Baroness Staffe, when she wrote in 1894: "Sophisticated Russians blend their boxed tea with apple blossom, the extremely mellow flavour of which adds to the excellence and fine quality of the leaf, which delights without intoxicating".

"The first tea cups were made in Cronstadt. Well, it often came about that, for reasons of economy, the café owners would put less tea in the teapot than was actually required. So, as a view of Cronstadt was depicted on the bottom of the cup, which the transparency of the liquor left too clearly visible, the consumer called over the merchant and, showing him the bottom of the cup, said: "You can see Cronstadt". Therefore, as the merchant could not deny that you could see Cronstadt, and as, if the tea was strong enough, you should not be able to see Cronstadt, the merchant was caught red-handed, committing fraud. On account of which, the merchant had the idea of substituting glasses, on the bottom of which nothing could be seen, for the cups, where you could see Cronstadt."

Alexandre Dumas,
Le grand dictionnaire de cuisine

Wild apple blossom was preferred. Tea is drunk sweetened with sugar, although some people prefer jam, eating it with a small spoon. The Russians often serve tea with slices of lemon, which is why lemon tea is sometimes called *Russian tea*. Tea is rarely served with milk.

Tea in Central Asia

Turkmen, Kirghiz, Mongols: Tea has long been the favourite drink of these nomadic peoples of the steppes of Asia, who are protected against the rigours of the climate by their felt-covered yurts.

Opposite page, bottom left
Piala, the traditional tea bowls of Uzbekistan.

MONGOLIAN TEA SOUP

Set up at the centre of the tent, perpendicular to the smoke hole that lets in the light, the hearth is fuelled by charcoal or by dried yak dung. Above the embers, a bronze tripod supports a bell-shaped copper cauldron containing the tea. Thick and greasy, this tea looks more like soup. It is an ancient custom. As long ago as 1865, in an article in the *Tour du Monde*, and taking his inspiration from the notes made by the French consul in China, M. de Bourboulon, A. Poussielgue wrote: "The Chinese, who make green tea expressly for the Europeans, since they won't use it themselves at any price, make block tea for the Mongols using the coarsest leaves and the slender sprigs of this precious bush; this mixture, pressed and compounded in a mould, takes on the shape and thickness of the terra cotta bricks used for their buildings. The poor Siberians also drink this cheap tea, which is much less pleasant than the other, but which, when combined with some milk and barley flour, forms a thick and nourishing gruel called *pan-tan* […]".

TEA FOR ANY TIME

Alongside fermented sheep's milk, tea actually plays an important nutritional role. In the past, a good fifteen varieties of tea were transported from China by caravan, making for a difficult choice in the bazaars: "The buyer would start by nibbling a single leaf, which he had soaked in water. If he liked the texture and flavour, he ordered a bowl of tea made with a pinch of leaves, which he tasted", explain Helen and George Papashvily. To each season, its tea. For each circumstance, the variety considered most appropriate… In the morning, block tea was combined with milk and a sprinkling of salt. Other times lent themselves "to *lonka*, a tea from eastern China so perfumed that a single leaf sufficed for one bowl of tea".

UZBEKISTAN, TADZHIKISTAN, KIRGHIZISTAN…

People in these countries drink tea throughout the day. As in Russia, the samovar punctuates daily life. There are many teahouses *(tchaïkhana)* where, reclining on low dais, men debate endlessly, a bowl of tea in their hands. It is the preserve of the male. As for the women, they drink their tea at home.

Tea in Kirghizistan

"It looks nothing like the tea we have in Europe: it is a real soup, prepared with milk, flour, butter and salt. In every well-to-do *aoul* (encampment or village), the women always have a pot full of this beverage over the fire, offering it first to visitors, in the same way as in Turkey they offer tea or in Spain chocolate."

Arthur Mangin, *Le Désert et le Monde sauvage*, 1866

Nutritious Tibetan tea

In mountainous countries, tea (boeja) is real, warming comfort food. It is made following a special recipe that is second to none.

Top right
A Tibetan tea block

Below
Lamasery, After a 19th-century engraving

TESTIMONY OF THE GREAT TRAVELLERS

In her *Voyage d'une Parisienne à Lhassa*, Alexandra David-Neel makes frequent mention of "Tibetan tea, buttered and salted, a soup rather than a beverage, perhaps, but a delicious cordial for the traveller that is tired and chilled to the bone". Together with *tsampa*, this tea was her staple food during the long and hard voyage she made across unexplored regions, accompanied by her adopted son, Lama Yongden. More recently, Fosco Maraini (*Tibet Secret*, 1952) describes the tea ritual on the Roof of the World: "Sönam brings me a jade cup with a lid in the shape of a pagoda, on a curious silver saucer shaped like a lotus: I raise the lid and the young man begins to pour from a finely worked copper teapot this drink that the Tibetans call tea. […] I drink a few mouthfuls of my tea drink (butter, soda, salt, boiling water and tea all blended together in a bamboo cylinder) and I accept a few fried biscuits, greasy, covered in fluff, which I have great difficulty swallowing […]."

A SPECIAL MIXTURE

The Tibetans drink tea all day long. They use block tea, leaving it to boil for a long time before combining it with a little butter and salt in a sort of churn. They often serve it in wooden cups and say an offertory prayer before

drinking it. When drinking it, they try to keep back as much of the butter that floats on the surface of this drink so as to be able to mix with it a little *tsampa*, the principal dish of Tibet, and inseparable from tea. It is made from toasted barley flour. Every household must have some available, prepared less than nine days previously. As Fosco Maraini explains, "To eat it, you take a handful, which you place in the little bowl in front of you, after which you pour on a sufficient quantity of hot tea and mix it using your fingers to make a dough the consistency of fresh marzipan. Then, of course, you add some butter, again using the fingers. Finally, you eat it a little bit at a time. Disgusting? A thousand times better than the terrible muck given such fancy French names that they serve up in Indian restaurants!"

Left
The Dalai Lama, the most famous Tibetan, is a tea lover.

In Nepal

Following the example of the Tibetans, the Nepalese drink tea with salt and yak butter. They like it piping hot and sweet. That is how it is served along the mountain roads and paths in the little village cafés, known here as *chia pazal* or 'tea houses'.

Left
A warming, comforting drink of tea under canvas in Tibet.

Sophisticated Oriental tea

All the countries of North Africa drink it, Morocco even more so than Algeria and Tunisia. It is prepared using only top-quality green tea and derives its special flavour from mint.

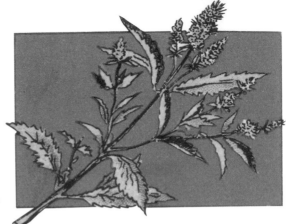

Fresh mint (top right) is used. The mint from Tiznit in southern Morocco is considered to be the best because it is very fragrant.

THE RITUAL OF MAKING TEA

The teapot is first rinsed with boiling water. The tea is added and a glass of boiling water poured over it to remove its bitterness, then the water is discarded. Then comes the mint, previously rubbed between the hands to release its aroma, followed by the sugar cubes (12 to 14 for three teaspoons of tea and 750 ml water). Boiling water is then poured on top and stirred with a spoon. The tea must be left to infuse for five to six minutes, before being served piping hot in the small, decorated glasses reserved for this drink.

TEA IN MOROCCO

In Morocco, the first tea of the day is drunk without mint. The second tea is made with mint: mint is added to the teapot where the tea has infused, followed by a teaspoon of tea and one of sugar. It is then filled up with boiling water and left to infuse. Before being served, it is again stirred with a spoon.

AROMATIC ADDITIONS

Often, a spoonful of perfumed water (such as orange flower water or rose water, for example) is added to

Glasses and teapot are placed on a large copper tray, chased in varying degrees, and supported by turned wooden feet. Alongside, on a smaller tray, the metal boxes containing the green tea, mint and aromatic herbs, as well as the sugar lumps.

"Lalla Aïcha [...] slipped out for a second to go to her kitchen to get the copper kettle and the brazier. The ready-prepared tray held centre-stage in the room. A gold embroidered veil covered it. Beneath it, showing through, I noticed the pewter teapot and the glasses. [...] She quickly stood up, went to find the sugar and the mint. My mother launched into a recital of her memories of the weddings she had attended. The tea was prepared in record time. Lalla Aïcha served everyone. She handed me my glass with two fingers of tea in the bottom. I protested. I asked for a well-filled glass like I had at home."

Ahmed Sefrioui,
La Boîte à merveilles, 1954

the infusion with the boiling water. The tea can also be flavoured by adding a few orange flowers or a sprig of basil, marjoram or verbena. It is considered the height of sophistication to plunge balls of amber, whether ambergris or black amber, into the tea for a few minutes. Finally, a few lightly roasted pine nuts or, less extravagantly, unsalted roasted peanuts, can be sprinkled over the glass of mint tea.

Tea with the Sultan

"The tea was served above the second fountain, on a table laden with silverware, where the hundred wonders of Maghreb patisserie were spread out, gazelle horns, honey flaky pastries, judge's turbans, almond-flavoured milk, beverages flavoured with squeezed orange, lemon or raspberries, the champagne that their religion tolerates as an innocent sparkling water. In front of enormous Muscovite samovars, which all of a sudden bring to mind the idea of snow and wintry weather in this land of light, servants made the tea in accordance with the kaida."

Jérôme and Jean Tharaud,
Rabat ou les Heures marocaines

THE TEAPOT GAME FOR MAKING 'TOUAT TEA'

In south-west Algeria, a whole set of body movements is involved. One teapot, which has been placed on the heat for five minutes, contains the tea and the boiling water; another contains the sugar and the mint leaves. The tea from the first teapot is poured into the second. Then a glass is filled, and its contents poured into the teapot. This operation has to be repeated three or four times until the sugar is completely dissolved.

THE DRINK OF THE SAHARA

Tea is everywhere in the desert. Green tea, which is thought to have reached the Sahara by sea during the 18th century, is now one of the main commodities of Saharan trade, along with the traditional block of sugar that is broken into pieces. As Théodore Monod explains in *Méharées* (1989): "Small teapots, tiny glasses. A bitter concoction in the first glass, then sickly sweet, syrupy.

The liturgical 'tour' comprises three glasses, sometimes four. The mixture is sometimes flavoured with mint, *gartoufa* (an aromatic mixture), clove, lavender, even pepper".

Obviously, the number of glasses varies depending on the wealth of the hosts. This ritual of the three dedicated glasses that you drink while conversing is called *timia* by the Tuaregs. The tea is generally served with a piece of pancake cooked in the ashes or even the desert sand. The pancake is served as it comes or moistened with sweetened sheep's milk, or even unsweetened whey. According to another 'recipe', described by Monod, "the *kessera* is broken up into crumbs, powdered and combined using the hands with a sauce made from sugar, tea, butter, dried apricot paste etc. A dish of this paste, preceded by three small glasses of tea and followed by a litre of *guerba* water, makes a substantial meal".

Previous page
A glass of tea in the desert: an expression of hospitality.

Top
Salon in a Tartar house in Shoucha.

Tea with a Tartar

"When we arrived at the home of this Tartar, we found there a large company; the salon was not large, but I liked its elegance. It was full of guests seated along the walls; to judge from their faces, you would think they were absorbed in the deepest of reflections; their beards were black and red, they had a piece of amber in their mouths and a hookah in their hand. These hookers were passed from hand to hand.

We were served a light meal consisting of tea and pilau (rice cooked with butter or fat and meat and strongly spiced) that they sprinkled with tea."

Basile Vereschaguine,
Voyage dans les provinces du Caucase, 1864-65

Below
Archives relating to the import of tea by boat.

A treasure-trove of tea

To gather in one place teas from all the world, to make this place into a real teahouse, with the charm of the colonial trading posts… all in the heart of Paris was the challenge the Mariage brothers set themselves.

In the 18th century, Jean-François Mariage ran a tea, spice and colonial foodstuffs business in Lille. His four sons trained at the business school. It was therefore totally logical that, in about 1820, Louis, Aimé and Charles succeeded their father as head of the Lille business.

The Paris store
In 1845, Aimé and Auguste Mariage founded the firm of Auguste Mariage et Compagnie in Rue du Bourg-Tibourg, Paris, a company steeped in the family tradition.

A family dedicated to trade
The commercial calling of the Mariage family began long ago. A member of a delegation chosen by Louis XIV and the East India Company to sign a commercial treaty with the Shah, Nicholas Mariage discovered Persia and India in about 1660. His brother, Pierre, meanwhile, was the same company's 'ambassador' to Madagascar.

This was the first stage in the development of a Parisian establishment that would result in 1854 in Aimé's sons, Henri (1827–1907) and Édouard (1828–1890), founding the famous Mariage Frères teahouse, which would go on to become the leading French tea importer. Today, it sells over 450 types of tea from 32 countries. "A scent of adventure and romance escapes towards infinity from each cup of tea", declared Henri Mariage. This idea of tea remains, at the turn of the 21st century, the guiding thread of the Mariage Frères company. The first retail establishment having opened in the 1980s, they have now expanded to other places, as far as Japan, where it started up with the aim of spreading the word about the 'French art of tea'.

A tea museum

Created in 1991 in the décor retained from its parent company, the Musée du Thé Mariage Frères in Paris brings together ancient objects that illustrate the history of tea: various containers used to transport and sell tea, boxes intended to preserve it, teapots ancient and modern. Precious woods and rare porcelain, silver and ivory attest to the sophistication that has continued to surround the enjoyment of this beverage through the centuries.

Variations on the theme of tea

As well as being a traditional drink, tea has proved to have numerous other talents. While it often provides the main ingredient in some other drinks, giving them a lift with its wonderful aroma, it also pops up in unlikely looking places, where it is used for aesthetic, even domestic reasons.

Let's start with tea

As we have already seen, the recipe differs from one place to another. In one place, the addition of half a vanilla pod gives tea a Creole note, while elsewhere the infusion is made replacing half the tea leaves with orange blossom.

The spiciest spirits go well with tea, to the even greater delight of tea lovers.

A REMEDY FOR WINTRY WEATHER

In the 19th century, Baroness Staffe tells us, the Scandinavians would drink tea mixed with red Bordeaux wine in equal measure to produce an extremely 'warming' drink. The same can be said of the Russian version, where vodka is poured into the cup before adding the hot tea. And vice versa: some people flavour vodka with tea *(tchaïnaia)*; the simplest recipe involves adding to a vodka bottle a tea bag that has already been soaked in a little boiling water, leaving it to infuse for five or six hours in a cool place, before straining.

Equally comforting is whisky tea, which will contribute greatly to the friendly cheer of a winter's evening. Simply pour two tablespoonfuls of whisky into each glass, then top up with very strong, sweet tea and a few slices of orange and lemon. Teetotallers can be served a honey tea: for a really invigorating drink, just put a teaspoonful of honey and two of sugar in each cup, then top with a fairly thick slice of lemon before pouring on the unsweetened, piping hot tea!

Tea liqueur

"Take 125 grams of good imperial or green tea and infuse it in half a litre of boiling water. When this first infusion is no more than lukewarm, you will have a strong tincture, which you then pour, together with the tea leaves, into 8 litres of brandy or spirits of wine diluted, […] with ordinary water; seal the jug with a tight-fitting stopper and leave to macerate for 8 days. […] Then it is distilling time. This operation is achieved by heating the liqueur in a bain-marie until a strong flow results for the first 4 litres that it produces. The process is then repeated; and, having lowered the heat, we continue with the distillation at a trickle to obtain 4 litres and a half. Next make the cold syrup, by melting 2 kilograms and a half of sugar in 4 litres and a half of water; combine with the tea spirit and filter."

Les Secrets du liquoriste et du confiseur, End of the 18th–beginning of the 19th century

Tea brandy

"Brandy: 5.5 litres; river water: 2.7 litres; imperial tea: 30 grams; crushed sugar: 2 kilograms.

Infuse the tea in the brandy for 8 days, then draw off 3 litres of liqueur by means of distillation; dissolve the sugar in the water, combine the two and filter. Much less tea is required if making tea brandy by means of infusion, but the liqueur will be yellow rather than clear and does not look so good."

Les Secrets du liquoriste et du confiseur,
End of the 18th–beginning of the 19th century

Tea cocktails

Tea goes well with fruit juices (such as orange, lemon and pineapple) and with some cordials (pomegranate, strawberry and raspberry, for example). When it comes into contact with fruit (such as orange, lemon and lime), it absorbs the fruit flavour. It also goes well with flavourings such as ginger, cloves, nutmeg or cinnamon. Barmen combine it with rum, cognac, brandy, champagne, Curacao, Grand Marnier and arrack to mention but a few. As for the famous punch (see following page), whether hot or cold, there are a thousand and one ways of making it. Tastes vary, green tea sometimes being preferred to black tea, dark rum to white rum and brown sugar to white caster sugar.

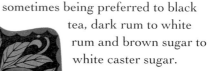

In the 19th century, in some literary works, tea served with a slice of lemon is called 'American tea'. But the Americans are not the only ones to drink it that way!

Tea punch of times gone by

Punch gets its name from the Hindi word panch, (meaning 'five'), as it was originally made up of five ingredients: a spirit, a liqueur or wine; milk; water or an infusion; sugar; and a flavouring.

A festive flame on a bed of orange slices!

AT THE HEART OF AN EVENING PARTY

Punch was very much in fashion during the 19th century, so much so that it lent its name to the gathering at which it held centre-stage. A number of testimonies have been handed down to us relating to its presence at intellectual and literary gatherings, where it warmed the body and the mind. Unlike the beverage we know today, in the past it was usually a drink that kept well and was therefore prepared in advance and reheated just before serving. Again, unlike modern-day recipes, punch was usually made using tea as its base, to which were added lemon, sugar and rum. There were countless variations on this basic recipe.

SIROP de CITRON

QUALITÉ SUPÉRIEURE

ESSENTIAL EQUIPMENT: THE PUNCH BOWL

Punch was served hot in glasses from the large bowl in which it was brought to the table. When he was staying in New York, the French gourmet and lawyer, Brillat-Savarin (1755–1826), was able to drink punch in a café-bar. "Little himself", he wrote, "brought us a *bowl* of it, probably prepared in advance, which would have served 40 people. We simply don't have bowls of that size in France." However, in *Les Jeunes-France*, Théophile Gautier devotes a story to the *Punch Bowl*: "A punch bowl, as big as the crater of Vesuvius, was deposited on the table by two of the least inebriated members of the group.

Its flame rose at least three or four feet high, blue, red, orange, violet, green, white – a dazzling sight.

A draught, coming from an open window, made it flicker and tremble; one would have said it was the tail of a salamander or a comet. […]

The lights were extinguished; we could see no less clearly.

The glow of the bowl extended throughout the room, and penetrated right into the furthest recesses. One could have believed oneself in the fifth act of a modern play, when the hero rises up to heaven, or at the gallows at the centre of the Bengal fires. […]

The punch was served piping hot in glasses, which cracked and crackled with a dry sound. In less than quarter of an hour, it was all gone, and total darkness reigned in the room."

Liqueur punch

In a saucepan, put 10 grams of green tea, 1 kilo of sugar lumps and 1 litre of water. Add the zest of 4 lemons and 3 untreated and unpeeled oranges, cut into slices. Bring to the boil, then strain the contents of the saucepan and stir in 2 litres of dark rum.

Another recipe suggests putting 1 teaspoon of tea, the zest of 1 lemon, the flesh of that lemon, cut into slices and pips removed, and 375 grams of caster sugar into a container. Pour over 1 litre of boiling water, then leave to infuse for about 20 minutes before adding 500 millilitres of brandy. Mix well and strain before bottling

Summery iced tea

Tea is an excellent thirst-quencher, whether served hot or cold, but during hot summer days some people prefer to offer their guests an easy-to-prepare iced tea.

A taste of summer

"And the strawberries! Moisten them with the juice of the orange, of course. You can add the flesh of the orange, or give them a lift by whisking them with a little sugar; that's even better. It's simply divine if you add a few drops of a chilled, strong orange pekoe tea."

Maurice Germa,
in *"La Cuisinière poétique"*
Charles Monselet, 1859

THE RULES OF THE ART
"Cold tea is one of the most refreshing summer drinks, provided it is served without sugar or milk. Make it first thing in the morning. It must be very strong, but should not infuse for too long. Leave it in a stoneware jug until it is time to serve it, with slices of lemon or pineapple and small pieces of crushed ice in the glass", wrote Baroness Staffe in 1894.

DEPENDING ON WHEN THE TEA IS TO BE SERVED
In actual fact, the method used to prepare iced tea varies depending on whether the

drink is intended for immediate consumption or to be enjoyed later. If the tea is to be served immediately, simply make an infusion of tea in the usual way, pour this hot tea over the ice placed in a pitcher, add sugar and milk to taste – or sugar and lemon (juice and slices) – and flavour with a few drops of rum. This iced tea can also be made straight in the glass, pouring the ingredients over a few ice-cubes or crushed ice.
If the tea is not going to be served immediately, it can be kept in the refrigerator. In this case, make the infusion, then remove the leaves and add the sugar. Add the milk or lemon, or rum if using, just before serving.

Previous page
Orange goes
beautifully with
chilled tea.

Right
A holiday tea:
put an ice-cube
in a glass and
pour over a
quarter-glass of
reasonably
strong, cold,
sweetened tea,
followed by half
a glass of
pineapple juice, a
little soda water
and a dash of
lemon juice.

A RECIPE FOR SUCCESS

Whichever recipe you use, it
is essential to use hot (40 °C),
rather than boiling water to
prevent the drink from
becoming cloudy, and to leave
it to infuse for an hour or
more. Another tip to help iced
tea retain its flavour is to fill
an ice-cube tray with tea and
to place it in the freezer until
frozen. These ice-cubes will
be invaluable when making
iced tea.

New beverages

Alongside the unchanging tradition of tea, the end of the 20th century saw the appearance of some new beverages on the market. They may be industrially produced, but they are no less an indication of how an age-old product has been adapted to suit changing tastes.

A SPARKLING ALLIANCE

The fashion for tea-based drinks has given rise to creations that are often very original in concept. Thus, in 1995, in response to the demand from a Swiss nightclub for a sparkling, subtle and non-alcoholic drink, Henri Bellot, a cider producer in Chaource, France, came up with the idea of blending cider and dessert apples from his region (the Pays d'Othe), with tea leaves, a little caffeine and a natural fruit flavour to produce a lightly sparkling, refreshing and thirst-quenching drink. He called it *Goldnight*, packaged it in a Champagne-type bottle and launched it in 1998.

Following in the footsteps of traditional cordials, the end of the 1990s saw the appearance of a tea cordial flavoured with lemon, peach or other fruits, or even cider, as used by Bellot.

READY TO SERVE

The United States has long known *ice tea*, whereas Europe did not discover it until the 1970s. Twenty years later, this product saw a remarkable growth, due without a shadow of doubt to the collaboration, at a global level, between the tea giants and the refreshing drinks multi-nationals.

In small and large bottles, even packs and cartons, iced tea swept through Europe. Switzerland proved to be the largest consumer (38 litres *per capita* per year), way ahead of Austria, Italy, Belgium and Germany, with France trailing behind at only 1.6 litres *per capita* per year. Estimated European sales for 2000 came to over 2,500 million litres! The quest for a healthier life goes a long way to explaining the success of this refreshing drink, sparkling or still, made with a tea base and flavoured (with lemon, peach, mint to mention but a few). The advertising also emphasises the natural and tonic properties of this ready-made tea, recommended to athletes.

Une nouvelle génération se présente ...

óPfanner
ICE TEA
PREMIUM

This slightly sweetened Austrian iced tea is made from an infusion of Ceylon or Assam tea and a dash of peach juice.

False teas

The word 'tea' was often used to describe drinks that had nothing in common with real tea apart from the method of preparation. In France, therefore, in times gone by, an infusion made of herbs such as lemon balm and sage to remedy gastric complaints used to be called *French tea* or *indigenous tea*. *Alpine tea* or *Swiss tea*, "made from flowers picked from Swiss balm plants", was, according to Alfred Franklin, "superior to Indian tea for the use and the properties explained on each box".
The *red tea* from South Africa, made from a plant called the *Rooibosch* (red bush), is no more related to tea than the famous *maté* of South America.

Riquet-Tee

kräftig aromatisch

South American tea

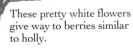

In the past, the Indians used to chew the leaves of the Ilex paraguariensis, a shrub that grew wild in the wooded regions of Paraguay. It then became customary to use them to make an infusion…

THE SOUTH AMERICANS' FAVOURITE 'LIQUEUR'
The infusion was nicknamed 'Paraguayan tea', 'Jesuit tea', and also called 'St Bartholomew's herb'. When telling of his *Journey around the World* (1771), Louis Antoine de Bougainville mentioned maté or 'Paraguay herb'. In the 19th century, maté was exported in great quantities to other Latin American countries, such as Peru, Chile, Argentina and some provinces in Brazil. Consumption was considerable. People drank it as soon as they got up and at any time of the day from then on. It was simply inconceivable to travel without it. The Europeans liked it a lot too, actually introducing it to Europe during the course of the last quarter of the 19th century.

A STIMULATING DRINK
The harvest, which begins in December, continues for some nine months. The leaves are dried, roasted and then ground to a powder. Over time, this pale green powder develops its flavour, which is similar to tea. Its leaves contain a small amount of theine, so the infusion is a stimulant, provided that it is weak, because it quickly becomes an irritant if too strong. All of which explains why it was used in Europe during periods when trade restrictions were in place.

Above
The vase used for the infusion called maté by the Spanish and culha by the Brazilians has now been replaced by a small, simply or ornately decorated gourd.

Far left
The *bombilla*, a sort of straw, made of wood or metal (usually silver) is used to suck the drink into the mouth.

These pretty white flowers give way to berries similar to holly.

The maté harvest in Paraguay in the 19th century.

As a result, some cookery books published during the Second World War recommended 'maté pampero'. "It is similar to coffee in flavour, but is made in exactly the same way as tea, and has the same properties of nervous over-stimulation. It is fortifying, uplifting and recommended for people who need a powerful tonic", attests Marcelle Daguin (*Recettes de cuisine et conseils ménagers*, 1940).

THE MATÉ RITUAL

Today, maté (or *yerba maté*) is still widely consumed in Paraguay, Uruguay and in some regions of Chile. Brazil is a major producer, while Argentina is the largest consumer. Usually served in a gourd, maté is generally drunk 'neat', although some people prefer to add sugar and cream.

Several versions

"To make the American beverage, put some sugar and a live coal in a vase intended for this sole purpose. Toast the sugar slightly, then add a varying amount of powder. Pour on very hot, but not boiling water [...]. The inhabitants of the countryside, day labourers and all men in general take *maté cimarrou*, in other words without sugar; but women and foreigners add coffee, rum, a little orange or lemon peel, while others use milk instead of water."

Alfred Demersay,
Le tour du monde, 1865

Tricks with tea

Our grandmothers knew them well and put them into practice. We have often lost all memory of them. Yet they have been successfully tried and tested…

Right
Common knowledge to lace makers, tea delicately dyes their precious work, turning it a very attractive colour.

Tea in the kitchen

• **Rub a frying pan with damp tea leaves to remove stubborn odours, such as onion or fish.**
• **Soaking in tea rather than the usual water increases the flavour of dried fruits.**
• **There again, why not use tea to deglaze a frying pan that has just been used to cook a piece of meat? The gravy will taste all the better for it.**

DELICATE DYES
Tea turns out to be effective in many different fields. Even its staining properties can be turned to good effect. So, to turn strips of lace an attractive ochre colour, just soak them in a strong tea mixture, then roll them up and leave them for an hour before ironing while still damp, taking care to stretch them out thoroughly. For a paler colour, just wring them out and leave them to dry flat, before ironing while still damp.

IN THE HOUSE
Tea is a useful cleaning agent. A cold infusion makes mirrors or chrome gleam and cleans painted panelling. It is also good for bringing dark-coloured carpets and rugs back to life: just brush them with infused tea leaves that have been squeezed dry, then go over the carpet or rug with the vacuum. Tea can also be used to feed house plants. They will thrive on a potting medium made of a mixture of infused tea leaves and soil, followed by an occasional watering with a tea infusion.

TO REMOVE TEA STAINS

There is nothing more
annoying than a white
tablecloth that bears the
hallmark of a friendly gathering
over a cup of tea! A few drops
of lemon juice will remove the
stain, but take care to rinse it
out in cold water afterwards.
On a coloured tablecloth, the
stain will disappear if you apply
egg yolk thinned down with
warm water. This also works
for woollen or silk fabrics. Nor
do tea stains on carpets or rugs
present an insurmountable
problem. A mixture of equal
parts of methylated spirits and
dry white wine (or white
vinegar) will see to them; it is
best to soak the carpet with the
mixture, then press down
forcefully with a dry cloth.
Finally, there is just one
solution for an old stain: water
mixed with glycerine.

FOR BEAUTY'S SAKE

"Weak tea, black tea is good for bathing painful eyes", as recommended by Baroness Staffe in 1891 in her *Cabinet de Toilette*, and subsequently confirmed a few decades later, in her own way, by A. Villeneuve in her *Secrets de beauté*: "Shadow under the eyes, if it is indeed beautiful at all, can be obtained without the use of any cosmetics by applying lotions of strong tea. In the same way as infusions of walnut leaves, tea can only strengthen the eyesight, both being rich in tannins."
In addition to these properties that are at one and the same time soothing and stimulating for the eyes, tea, so says the same Baroness, lends itself to

"Tea can be smoked in the same way as Tobacco, after lightly moistening the leaves by sprinkling a spoonful of brandy over them like dew; & the sediment or ash that remains at the base of the pipe is marvellous for whitening the teeth", as Massialot attested at the end of the 17th century.

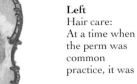

Left
Hair care:
At a time when
the perm was
common
practice, it was
recommended to
moisten the hair
with tea before-
hand so that the
curls would hold
better.

inoffensive hair-dyes. If very strong, "it is quite
good at dyeing blond hair that is turning light
brown". A more original recipe consists of putting
nails in the tea and leaving them there for a
fortnight to produce a dark dye! Be that as it may,
there is no denying that rinsing brown hair in tea
gives it shine and coppery highlights. With its
indisputable beneficial properties, tea can also be
used to make an excellent lotion for greasy skins
(three tablespoons of leaves for 500 millilitres of
mineral water). Some people even recommend
adding a few drops of lemon juice.
Finally, tea was also reputed to prepare the
epidermis for a summer tan, which it would then
prolong.

The gastronomy of tea

Taking tea is a pretext for precious moments where biscuits, cakes and sweetmeats have pride of place. It sometimes happens, however, that recipes develop around tea which highjack the flavour for other such epicurean delights…

result, and combined with the talent of various chefs, the drink has become a culinary ingredient in its own right. Admittedly, this phenomenon is not new. As long ago as 1742, there was a recipe for tea ice-cream written by Father Labbat. A much

appreciated dessert in the 19th century, tea cream features in all the cookery books of the time, as do milk tea eggs, compotes with tea, tea-flavoured pancakes or desserts and pastries based on prunes flavoured with tea (generally Ceylon or Indian).

Western concoctions

Over the last few decades of the 20th century, a tea art developed in the West that is more attentive to the subtleties of its estates and flavours. As a

Above
Tea soup:
Butter some slices of bread and use them to line a soup tureen; sprinkle with sugar; pour over one glass of strong tea and two of milk.
La Cuisinière de la campagne et de la ville, L.-E. Audot 1841.

BISCUITS OLIBET

Nowadays, however, its gastronomic uses have multiplied: tea is used to flavour sweets, chocolate fillings, jellies or mousses, and to give a lift to savoury dishes, particularly fish and poultry.

Japanese delicacies

Cherry, plum and rape flower in spring, carnations and convolvulus in summer, dead leaves, maple, chestnut and chrysanthemum leaves in autumn, snow crystals, bamboo nodes and camellias in the depths of winter: Japanese delicacies change shape and colour with the seasons. Some of these delicacies, the *wagashi*, leave nothing to chance or the imagination. Both in its appearance, which gives it a message, and in its manufacture, which continues to be by craftsmen and almost religious in nature, the biscuit fastidiously respects a tradition that is almost two thousand years old, having developed with the Buddhist and Shinto religions before it was linked with the tea ceremony. Nowadays, this malleable sweetmeat, whose pastry base is generally made from a fine flour produced from ground, toasted rice which is then combined with water and a little cane sugar, is served with unsweetened green tea. Placed on the tongue before or after the ritual drink, it brings sweetness to this manifestation of the Japanese art of living.

Appendices

❖

A few recipes

For breakfast:

For breakfast, the Japanese sometimes eat *cha-gayu*, a sort of tea porridge renowned for its digestive properties.

• Pour 1 cup of rice into a saucepan and add 7 cups of a weak infusion of green Bancha tea. Bring to the boil over a high heat, then immediately lower the heat.

• Leave to cook for at least 40 minutes, stirring only at the end of this cooking time. Then add a little salt, cover and leave to rest for a few minutes before serving.

Escalope of Salmon with Matcha

Mariage Frères Recipe

Serves 8

**8 x 6 oz salmon escalopes,
1 oz powdered green tea
(Matcha),
beurre manié (soft paste of
flour and butter),
1 scant cup crème fraîche,
juice of half a lemon,
4 cups fish stock,
table salt,
freshly ground white pepper.**

• Bring the stock to the boil, remove any scum with a slotted spoon, and take off the heat. Add the tea, then beat with a whisk. Bring back to the boil.

• Thicken the stock with the beurre manié. Stir in the cream and leave to reduce over a very low heat. Add the lemon juice and seasoning. Pass through a fine sieve and keep warm.

• Steam the salmon escalopes and arrange them on the plates. Coat with the hot sauce and serve immediately.

Chicken supreme with tea

Mariage Frères recipe

**6 chicken breasts,
2 oz Earl Grey tea,
butter, flour,
2 cups coconut milk,
chicken stock.**

• Bring 4 cups of water to the boil. Add 2–3 tbsps of chicken stock, then the tea, and infuse for 3–4 minutes. Strain through a fine sieve. Add the coconut milk, bring to the boil and simmer for a few seconds.

• Make a roux with the butter and flour, then gradually stir into the coconut milk mixture until it is smooth. Whisk, then set aside in a cool place.

• Cook the chicken breasts in some chicken stock for 10 to 15 minutes. Drain them, then slice finely. Arrange the chicken slices in a fan shape on a plate and garnish with parsley and baby vegetables.

Milk tea eggs

**6 eggs,
4 cups milk,
3 oz caster sugar,
2 teaspoons tea.**

• Boil the tea in 2 cups milk for 5 minutes. Strain the infusion and leave to cool.
• Combine the eggs with the tea-flavoured milk and the remaining unflavoured milk. Add the caster sugar, stirring constantly.
• Pour the mixture into an ovenproof dish and bake in a low oven for about 20 minutes, until golden on top. Serve in the dish.

Tea Cream

**2 oz Chinese tea,
2 cups cream
9 oz caster sugar,
3 eggs, separated.**

• Bring the cream to the boil, pour over the tea and leave to infuse for 30 minutes.
• Pass the cream mixture through a sieve, add the sugar, 3 beaten egg yolks, and lastly 1 egg white, whisked into stiff peaks.
• Leave to set in a bain-marie.

Sprinkle with sugar.
• Serve cold.

N.B. Another traditional recipe makes this cream using 1 tbsp black and green tea, mixed, 4 cups boiling milk, 9 oz sugar, 6 egg yolks (beaten) (or 2 egg whites whisked into stiff peaks).

A mild floral infusion

The Asians also use tea flowers, picked in bud and prepared in the same way as leaves; a sort of diet tea, as it is less rich in theine. They put one teaspoon of flowers per 2 cups water in a warmed teapot, then leave it to infuse for 20 minutes, before adding a few slices of fresh ginger. The flavour of this tea continues to increase even up to the second or third addition of water.

Tea 'liqueur' the old-fashioned way

"Soak 9 oz of top quality green tea in 2 cups boiling water and leave to macerate for half a day. Meanwhile, cook 2 lbs of sugar in 8 cups of rain water until the sugar is completely dissolved. Add an egg white to clarify the syrup and filter. Filter the tea too and then combine the two mixtures, bringing the temperature of the mixture down to 35° C by adding rain water; filter the mixture again and pour into clear glass bottles […], cork and seal the bottles, then keep them for one month exposed to light.
If a slight deposit should form in the bottles, decant them without filtering."

Marie-Anne de Cellay,
Crèmes, pâtisseries, bonbons et liqueurs de ménage, 1909

Infusion chart

	Quantity per cup	Water temperature	Infusion period
China and Formosa			
• White teas	2 tsps	70° to 85° C	15 min (Yin Zhen)
			7 min (Pai Mu Tan)
• Green teas	2 tsps	70° to 95° C	3 min
• Semi-fermented teas	1 tsp	95° C	7 min
• Black teas	1 tsp	95° C	5 min
India			
• Spring Darjeeling	1½ tsps	95° C	3 min
Other black teas			
• whole-leaf teas	1 tsp	95° C	5 min
• broken-leaf teas	1 tsp	95° C	3 min
• powdered-leaf teas	1 tsp	95° C	2 min
Blends of scented teas			
• black-tea based	1 tsp	95° C	5 min
• semi-fermented tea based	1 tsp	95° C	7 min
• green-tea based	1 tsp	95° C	3 min

(Provided by Mariage Frères)

Japanese green teas	Number of cups	Quantity of tea	Quantity of water	Infusion temperature	Infusion period
Sencha					
• ordinary *(medium grade)*	5	2 tsps	2 cups	90° C	1 min
• superior *(high grade)*	3	1 tsp	¾ cup	70° C	2 min
Gyukuro					
• ordinary *(medium grade)*	3	2 tsps	¼ cup	60° C	2 min
• superior *(high grade)*	3	2 tsps	¼ cup	50° C	2½ min
Bancha	5	3 tsps	3 cups	100° C	30 s
• Yanagi-cha					
• Genmai-cha					
• Hoji-cha					

(Taken from documents provided by the Japan Tea Exporters Association.)

Bibliography

BURGESS (R.) *The little book of tea*, Kansas City, 1998

CARLES (M.) AND BROCHARD (G.): *Plaisirs de thé*, Le Chêne, 1998.

DORJE (R.): *La Cuisine traditionnelle tibétaine*, L'Astrolabe, 1988.

FIGUIER (Louis): *Les Merveilles de l'industrie*, vol. 1, end of the 19th century.

FORTUNE (Robert): *A Journey to the Tea Countries of China*, London, 1852.

FRANKLIN (Alfred): *La Vie privée d'autrefois*, Plon, 1893.

LU YU: *Le Classique du thé*, 8thcentury, Republished by Morel, Apt, 1977.

MARIAGE FRÈRES: *L'Art français du thé*, Paris, 1999.

MÉTAILIÉ (Georges): *La Ronde des thés*, In "Terrain 13", October 1989.

PAPASHVILY (Helen and George): *The Art of Russian Cuisine*, Time-Life, 1969.

OKAKARA (K.): *The book of tea*, North Bay, 2003

PENNETIER (Dr Georges): *Leçons sur les matières premières*,

Paris, 1881.

RUNNER (Jean): *Tea*, « Que sais-je ? », 1970.

SCHAFER (C. & V.): *Teacraft*, San Francisco, 1975.

STAFFE (Baroness): *Traditions Culinaires* et *L'art de manger toute chose à table*, Paris, 1894.

STEINBERG (Rafael): *The Cooking of Japan*, Time-Life, 1969.

Les Secrets du Liquoriste et du Confiseur, end of 18th – beginning of 19th century l'Argonaute, Marseille, 1990.

Useful addresses

Specialist tea shops in Paris, France

• *Mariage Frères*
30-32, rue du Bourg-Tibourg 75004 Paris
13, rue des Grands Augustins 75006 Paris
260, Faubourg Saint-Honoré 75008 Paris

• *Le Palais des thés*
35, rue de l'Abbé Grégoire 75006 Paris
21, rue Raymond-Losserand 75014 Paris
21, rue de L'Annonciation 75016 Paris

• *La Théière*
118 bd du Montparnasse 75014 Paris

Specialist tea shops in London

• *Bramah Museum of Tea and Coffee*
40 Southwark Street, Bankside,
London SE1 1UN
• *The Drury Tea & Coffee Company*
Unit 15, Rich Industrial Estate,
Crimscott Street, London SE1 5UF
• *Whittard of Chelsea plc*
Brompton Road,
203/205 Brompton Road,
Knightsbridge, London SW3 1LA
Carnaby Street,
T-Zone, 43 Carnaby Street, London
W1F 7EA

Specialist tea shops in New York

• *Alice's Tea Cup*
102 West 73rd Street
• *Garden Court Café*
725 Park Avenue
USA online addresses:
The Guide to Tea Rooms and Tea
Shops in the USA, Canada, and
beyond ©: www.tearoomguide.info
Gladys Marie's Tea Shoppe & Gifts:
www.gladysmaries.com
Tea Association of the United States:
info@teausa.com

Photographic credits

All the documents reproduced in this book are from the author's own collection, except:
© Bellot: page 112 a. © Roland Beaufre: pages 29 a., 124 a. & b., 125. © Cedus: pages 65 b., 67, 108 b. © Comité français du thé / Olivier Scala: pages 27, 32 a., 36 b., 38 a., 41, 50 a. © Musée Dobrée in Nantes / Cl. Ch. Hémon: pages 10–11, 16 b., 52 b. © Explorer: pages 4, 30–31 & 34 (Lissac), 68 l. (Charmet), 76 (Perno), 78 b. (Baumgartner), 81 b. (Girard). © Christine Fleurent: pages 2, 3 r., 42 b., 44 a., 45 b., 49 a., 58 a., 59 a., 61 r. & l., 75 a. & b., 95, 102–103, 111, 122–123. © Musée Guimet: page 77 a.. © Photothèque Hachette: pages 19, 71, 85, 87 a., 98. © Stéphanie Leduc: pages 28, 39, 44 b., 50 bl., 50 br., 56 a., 57 r., 57 b., 74,bl., 89 b., 91 b. © Mariage Frères: pages 38 b., 45 a., 79 a., 100, 101 a., 116 b./ J-P Dieterlen: flyleaves, pages 1, 5 l. & br., 6, 17 l., 46, 48, 49 b., 51 b., 56 b., 59 b., 60 a., 65 a., 73 a., 79 a., 92 a., 120 b./ Bénédicte Petit: pages 37, 57 a., 62 a., 101 b. © François Ozon: cover, pages 54–55. © Pfanner: page 113 b. © Sygma: pages 82–83 (Laura Bosco), 93 ar. (P. Eranian), 93 b. (Valli-Summers). D.R.: pages 84 br. & bl., 87 b., 88.
a=above; b=below; l=left; r=right

Credits for cited texts

Page 28: Han Suyin, *La Montagne est jeune*, (*The Mountain is Young*), with the kind permission of Stock publishers.
Page 70: Michel Butor, *La Modification*, with the kind permission of Minuit publishers.
Page 72: John Blofeld, *Tea and Tao*, (*Thé et Tao, l'art chinois du thé*), translated by Josette Herbert, with the kind permission of Dervy publishers.
Page 89: Ahmed Sefrioui, *La Boîte à merveilles*, with the kind permission of Seuil publishers.
Page 92: Fosco Maraini, *Tibet secret*, with the kind permission of Flammarion publishers, Arthaud division.
Page 96: Théodore Monod, *Méharées* (1989), with the kind permission of Actes Sud publishers.

Any copyright holders whom the publisher, despite all their efforts, may not have been able to contact are invited to make themselves known.

First published by Editions du Chêne, an imprint of Hachette-Livre
43 Quai de Grenelle, Paris 75905, Cedex 15, France
Under the title *Le Thé*
© 1999, Editions du Chêne – Hachette Livre. All rights reserved

Language translation produced by Book Production Consultants plc, Cambridge

This edition published by Hachette Illustrated UK, Octopus Publishing Group Ltd.,
2–4 Heron Quays, London E14 4JP
English Translation © 2004, Octopus Publishing Group Ltd., London

Printed in Singapore by Tien Wah Press
ISBN 13: 978-1-84430-116-4
ISBN 10: 1-84430-116-8

The author is extremely grateful to Mr Kitti Cha Sangmanee, president of Mariage Frères, for the valuable assistance he has so willingly given. She would also like to thank Messrs. Christophe Bellot (Société Bellot, 10210 Chaource) and Bruno Wissler (Société Hermann Pfanner, Lauterach, Austria).

Editorial director: Colette Véron
Editing: Brigitte Leblanc
Art director: Sabine Houplain
Layout: Brigitte Racine